Pureheart

Seven Keys to Wholeness

PAMELA STANFIELD JACKSON

Copyright © 2013 Pamela S. Jackson

All rights reserved. No part of this book may be reproduced in any form or by any means without prior consent of the author, except in brief quotes used in reviews. To request more information in this matter send a request to pam-pureheart@carolina.rr.com.

Scriptures taken from the Holy Bible, New International Version © 2011-2013 unless otherwise noted.

Book Cover Design – Pamela S. Jackson

Revisions (May, 2013) – Dr. George B. Jackson

Photography (Back cover and inside) ~ Tamara N. Dix, Greensboro, NC

ISBN: 1484004264
ISBN-13: 978-1484004265

"He who has clean hands and a 'pure heart', who does not lift up his soul to an idol or swear by what is false; He will receive blessing from the Lord (Psalm 24:4-5 NIV).

Only a pure heart knows what is true

— Pamela S. Jackson

DEDICATION

I want to dedicate these words captured in this book to every person that will pick it up and that has asked the question why am I here?
I pray that My Heavenly Father Jesus the Christ will let something written on these pages encourage, inspire, and uplift you to seek the answer.

In loving memory of my mother Ardelia Dalton Stanfield who taught me by example how to love her God, her husband and her family. My mother did not do a Christian she was a Christian that exemplified with her life what it looked like to serve others.

In loving memory of my father Johnnie Earl Stanfield Sr. who taught me by example how to persevere no matter what and how not to start something that I could not complete.

I dedicate this book to the Stanfield and Jackson family because we are one - my husband Jack, our children (Marquis, Monica, Ashton, Phillip, and Martin), my siblings ~ Johnnie Jr., Jeremiah, Greg and my friend and sister Prissy!
To our godchildren, Toby, Antoine, Cameron (nephew) and Grant.

To all my girlfriends who have walked with me and stood by me even in the worst of times...this is dedicated to you.

Contents

Introduction	1
Chapter 1	5
Heal Spirit, Mind and Body	
Chapter 2	28
My Hidden Treasures	
Chapter 3	44
Pure Heart	
Chapter 4	66
Love the Center of my Joy	
Chapter 5	84
Laughter for the Soul	
Chapter 6	102
I Can, I Will, and I Must	
Chapter 7	116
Victorious	
Conclusion	129

i

Pamela S. Jackson

ACKNOWLEDGMENTS

I would like to first thank my Lord and Savior Jesus the Christ (Daddy) your love is amazing!
I thank you for loving me so much that you came where I was and asked me
"daughter do you want to be made whole"
even when my mouth couldn't answer your LOVE did!

I want to thank Dr. Janice Witt Smith for taking this manuscript with you on vacation and editing each page – I've carried it around for fourteen years.

I want to thank Bishop Dr. George B. Jackson (My Jack), The Citadel Ministries, honey I want to thank you for always believing in me. Your love is like rain in a dry land. I want to thank God for choosing me for you – prayerful I can *"helpmeet"* the work God has for us.

I want to thank Soul Care Ministries and the women that supports it…because of you I could complete this work

I want to thank the six ladies (each read a chapter for me) you gave me excellent feedback and you stated you wanted to read the entire book so here it is!

Preface
My Mommy

Every morning my mom would wake me up and start me off with my daily affirmations:
- I can do ALL things through Jesus Christ who strengthens me.
- I am a leader not a follower.
- I am the head and not the tail.
- I am above and not beneath.
- I am more than a conqueror.

My mom worked every day on building a daughter who was confident and comfortable in her own skin because her mother was also a strong confident woman who believed in raising strong God loving women.

My grandmother Ardelia, "*Nanny*" spent many days and nights in church; on prayer boards, in the choir, cooking Sunday meals for the Pastor. Her love for God and dedication for her family showed my mother how to start her own relationship with God. Other kid's played "Cowboys and Indians" or "Nurse", my mom and my Aunt Prissy played "Church". Maybe that is why I went to Monday Night Bible Study, Tuesday Night Bible Study, Wednesday Night Bible Study, Thursday Night Choir Practice, and three church services on Sunday. She stayed grounded in her beliefs because that's how she was raised.

She showed me how to selflessly help others because we were put on this Earth for so much more than we really know. She took me to soup kitchens, to shelters, to gatherings where we helped other kids get what they needed for school. She taught me to be kindhearted because there is no other way.

Pamela S. Jackson

People ask me all the time how I got to be the way I am, but when they meet my mother they instantly know. Self- expression through her vibrant styles, colors, and a cheery outlook was simply how I was raised. My mother has a special way of morphing the world around her so the troubles and the tarnish of the world don't even effect or faze her. She would probably call it *"God's shield of Righteousness"*. And you thought I'd forgotten all I had learned in Bible Study.

Ambitious and hardworking are two main words I would use to describe my mother. I remember she use to have a business card with like 5 different jobs listed on it: Wedding Planner, Event Coordinator, Flower Arrangements, Gift Baskets, Motivational Speaker, Basic Computer Skills for youth and seniors, and "Call for a kind word" (maybe not the last one professionally BUT we all know who to call if we need a spiritual pick me up). She's "Biblebull" instead of Redbull and I hope she continues to be unstoppable in her ministry.

I have so many wonderful memories of my mother. Some of my memories are simple things like us watching Diagnosis Murder and drinking hot tea every night before bed. Others are big life changers that helped mold me into who I am like taking me to plays and cultural diversity events. Even if we couldn't always afford it she would find a way because she knew the value of the experience was worth more than the money in her pocket.

I could speak for "24" years telling you how truly special she is to me. I consider it an honor to be from your womb, *"flesh of her flesh"*. Even if I wasn't your daughter, just knowing you is a blessing. You touch the lives of everyone you meet, you truly walk with God's light with love radiating and pouring out of you, just like Nanny did. I am so glad to call you my mother. I hope this year in 2013 everything you've been praying for takes root and sprouts. ~ *Ashton Vaughn for mommy's birthday 2-20-13*

Introduction

I started writing this book in 1999. Who would have thought it would have taken fourteen years to publish. I kept telling myself that I had not published this book because I could not put my hand on the last chapter. The other six chapters I had backed up on three or four devices and even found hard copies printed out but I could not find the seventh chapter anywhere. Finally I yielded to the Holy Spirit saying to me, *"just rewrite the chapter"*. Just rewrite the chapter. This is what this entire journey to wholeness has been about rewriting chapters in my life that did not speak the truth about me or my situation according to God's Word. So fourteen years later I rewrote the chapter. What you have now is me living through these seven chapters – 2 times (14 years) a double blessing.

I have had to forget some things, forgive some things, believe some things, and discover some things, but it has been worth the journey. The seventh chapter was going to be entitled *Self Esteem verses Spirit Esteem*. That is about all I recall about that. Most likely I had low self-esteem at the time and that was before I discovered I am a spirit and there is nothing missing or lacking with my spirit man. God is so amazing because He definitely did not want me to end this book on that note. But He wanted to end this book with transformation, revelation, and confirmation. When I think back fourteen years ago a lot has transpired. I was reminded of a dream today that I had in 1997.

> *I drove to an event that had lots of parked cars in front of the facility. When I arrived at the event there were orange cones reserving parking spaces and there was a parking attendant who waves me forward and he moves the orange cones for me to park close to the facility. I jump out of the car and it is a beautiful spring day as I head toward the facility. When I enter it seems I am in a museum and it's a line at this one main attraction. As I make my way through the crowd I realize it is a viewing of a glass coffin that has all the people intrigued. I move closer and there on display is a large glass coffin with two people inside. One was of a woman who sat close to the glass with her legs bent close up under her. She glanced up every now and then and even though she seemed lifeless there was a certain look in her eyes that told you that was not the case. The other one was an infant female child that crawled around the coffin and the lifeless woman. They both had ash grey faces with no coloring to signify ashes to ashes dust to dust. They were dressed likewise in ash grey sackcloth. When I approached the glass coffin something eerie*

stood out about the woman. Her eyes told the story..."Help me you could hear them say, help me...I'm not dead, can't you see me, help me. They have the lid on this coffin but I need to get me and my daughter out! There is not a lot of oxygen left in here and if I don't get out of here soon we will die". I moved passed her and moved pass the crowd to go back outside to find my car. But something about that woman disturbed my very being. I had to face the fact the woman inside the glass coffin for all to come observe was me!

I cried out to the Lord, Help me, save me, and my daughter! Once you cry out to the Lord to help you...He will! But let me explain further it does not involve others because He is changing you! If you are willing to be made whole please read these pages of not only my life experiences but some truths that will transform your thinking and revolutionize your life. To get a pure heart you first must acknowledge that you currently do not have one ! You must acknowledge that only the Lord really knows what is in your heart and what things have hampered your progress, have you bound, have you in a cycle, and have you thinking much to little of yourself than you ought!

Let me warn you it doesn't feel good…but it doesn't really have anything to do with feelings anyway. Once we know the truth even about our feelings it helps us to put things in perspective. I remember being peeled just like an onion, "oh not the big chunks of the onion, but the transparent skin layers" pulled back allowing light to pass through! The light is the "Word" of God and each time it pulls back layers He is trying to reveal truth! So I invite you to *"Pureheart: Seven Keys to Wholeness"*…A lot of things will not be new for you but to discover them through someone else's journey may help you understand you are not alone and there are specific principles to freedom.

Chapter 1
Heal Spirit, Mind and Body

Be transformed by the renewing of your mind
~ Romans 12:2

Are you tired of being tired? Are you looking for happiness and fulfillment in all the wrong places? We first must understand that we are a Spirit, we possess a Mind, and we live in a Body. Once we discover who we are, our purpose and direction become much clearer.

Who are you? Why are you here? Take a few minutes to think this over.

Have you attached yourself to attributes that you possess or positions that you hold, to determine who you are? Names do not tell us, they are only a way to distinguish one individual from another.

If names were who you are, since no two people are identical why would two people share names? Though your name may have some family significance, meaning and can symbolize characteristics that you possess, it still does not determine success or failure in your life.

Do you realize how imperative it is to know who you are? If you do not know who you are, how can you ever determine what you should be doing or where you should be going?

You will go through life aimlessly caught in the drama of being what you think you should be, or better yet what society has dictated for you to be. So to successfully be all you can be you must first determine who you are.

"People become what they are taught they can become. In order to deny people their basic human rights and needs, the first step is to deny them knowledge of who they are and fill that void with either wrong or negative knowledge."
~Author Unknown

Do you realize everything that is anything was in God in the beginning and God created everything that will exist in the beginning? That includes you, you were thought of in the beginning... that is an awesome concept. God knew how tall you would be, what color eyes, skin, and hair texture you would have, and how crooked that curve in your nose would

If you do not know who you are, how can you determine what you should be doing or where you should be going?

be. He knew how many hairs would be on your head, and what time of the day and year they each would turn gray or fall out. He knew exactly what year, day and time you would be born, and the year, day and time we each will die.

SPIRIT

Genesis 1:27 says, *"So God created man in His own image, in the image of God He created him; male and female He created them."*

You are created in the very image of God. (Do you know what image means here? The way you see something inside yourself...). This means God created you to be the way He saw Himself. All the attributes God has you have also... love, joy, peace, wisdom, power and on and on with no limitations.

God formed man's body from the dust of the ground. God spent time molding, making, shaping and smoothing out the rough spots in man as He formed him. God is the potter, you

♡ **God created us to be the way He saw Himself. All the attributes God has you have also... love, joy, peace, wisdom, power and on and on with no limitations.**

are the clay. He formed man's body with the earth. But you are not the body, it is only the container to house who you are. So you should not put more emphasis on the outward appearance than you do on your inward self which is your true identity.

Remember, the body is just dirt, (black dirt, white dirt, red dirt, yellow dirt, pink dirt, brown dirt, just dirt and when we die it returns to back to the earth from which it was created).. OKAY, let's get this established. Body, you are not who I am. *"And God breathed into his nostrils the breath of life; and man became a living soul."* The body only exists as long as the living soul needs a place to live.

We have to have the breath of God to be living – this is both physical and spiritual. Since we are made in God's image and God is "*Spirit*", His breath made us living '*spirits or living beings*' that reside in a dirt suit that He created for earthly purpose.

So you should transform your thinking from all the stigmas you have about the outside appearance. You are a living spirit created in the very image of God Himself (so the only true surgery that should be taking place is the one that you cannot see with the physical eyes and that is spiritual appearance). Where did you get sidetracked? Where did you lose your identity? Because if you knew who you truly were, nothing could ever make you feel less than what God's plan, image, and purpose is for you.

Since my profession is in the computer technology arena, I can say in computer terminology..."you need to defragment from the world's way of thinking and become reprogrammed to God's way of thinking".

You have heard the cliché what you see is what you get? Well what you see is not what you get! What you see is not who you are, it is just the body, which is housing who you are. And yes once you know who you are then the outward man must conform to its' rightful position. You are a *"spirit"* and you live in this body… Confess it, *"I am a living spirit."*

♡ **What you see is not who you are, it is just the body, housing who you are. And yes once you know who you are then the outward man must conform to its' rightful position. "I am a spirit and I live in this body …"**

Society has put so much emphasis on how a person looks. This is why a lot of people think they do not measure up; because they are evaluating outside in. There has been various "reality" TV shows that emphasize changing the outside appearances of people. When these individuals look at their appearances in the mirror after their cosmetic surgeries some are startled, shocked, and even confused by their new appearances. As they look in the mirror, they have problems accepting the new image they see, because their inner (image) spirit did not get a makeover so it is still at war.

It does not matter how much you do to the outward appearance if the inner self has not found peace you will not be satisfied with your outer self.

I had a beautiful friend that I met in 1999, I will call Grace. I was introduced to Grace from a ministry team from my church that visited individuals that were no longer able to attend church. When I met Grace I found her to be beautiful inside and out. But to convince Grace of this was going to be a different story! Grace had gone through a lot of abuse mentally, physically, and emotionally from a previous relationship. This abuse led her into a major depression which held her captive inside her body and inside her home. For years Grace never stepped foot outside of her home, but found comfort in eating, until she found herself faced with obesity in excess of 700 pounds and suffered from some major health problems. She faced what a lot of us go through and that is looking outside in. As a result to the pain and hurt that you encounter you feed the physical trying to find relief.

This is what society teaches, the flesh screams and hollers, so you feed it. Some feed it with food, drugs, and alcohol, some with sex, power, status, and with more things. You are constantly trying to satisfy a hunger within you that can never be satisfied with things on the outside or things of the flesh. These things are temporal anyway they will not last, neither will the body, the dirt that we so desperately try to please, it will not last it will all fade away.

Once Grace looked inside out, she realized she had dreams and aspirations that had not been fulfilled like all of us. She had to get beyond her fears and anxieties. And the biggest fear she had; was truly fear itself. She called me one night around 10:00 p.m. telling me how beautiful the sky was with the stars shining bright and the moon smiling back at her.

To some this sounds so trivial, but to her it was life. She had not stepped foot outside her home for over three years. May Grace rest in peace. She passed in 2007.

EMOTIONS

Emotions, senses and thoughts connected to our mind are the catalyst that stimulates the flesh.

Your Spirit was intended to use the emotions as sensors to discern between good and evil. Being physical beings you utilize the emotions to determine you want this or that based on how something feels to you.

You must realize that as physical beings your emotions have to rely on past experiences to be a measuring stick, because your physical being is not connected to an Omniscient (all knowing) God.

That privilege was lost in the Garden of Eden with the fall of man. So when you connect back to your Father then your emotions can also be connected back with Spirit and then

♡ ***Your spirit was intended to use your emotions as sensors to discern between good and evil.***

they can become measuring rods with the Spirit. They can prompt you when something just isn't right. (Not going on past experiences...but letting the All-knowing God, direct, guide and instruct your path of right...through discernment).

You have to learn to see from inside out, you have to hear from inside out, and you have to feel from inside out.

Once you let the flesh get involved, expect the wrong results and the wrong outcome. The two will never agree. *"That which is flesh is flesh and that which is Spirit is Spirit. The flesh can never understand the Spirit."* The flesh only imitates or duplicates what it can see, smell, taste, feel or hear. So trying to mix it with Spirit, which is connected with the All-knowing God, will always measure "I cannot compute and I do not agree."

That is why you cannot ask the flesh anything about you; it does not know and its answer will always be I cannot compute.

♡ ***Once you let the flesh get involved, expect the wrong results and the wrong outcome.***

The flesh is not who you are

The flesh will not admit it does not know but it will try to convince you otherwise. That is why it is fearful, it does not know. That is why it is always saying, "You cannot do this or that". That is why it is always saying "You do not measure up". That is why it is constantly screaming for attention. That is why it can be easily influenced from the outside and will try to redo and rework everything about your outside appearance in which God created. Try doing something that your spirit has revealed to you, and watch how your flesh will react... "NO, stop, quit, you cannot do it". Your flesh will say... "You do not know what you are doing and I am afraid", therefore you cannot be considering this. Well do not ask your flesh.

Let your spirit control as you are connected to the Holy Spirit. So you tell the flesh, "sit down and hush your mouth because "I can, I will and I must, do all things through Christ Jesus who strengthens me".

Tell the flesh, "you can only dig up things from my past; you do not know where I am going or how I will get there. Your purpose dirt suit is only to house me. So when I say go, just get to stepping, okay"!

You must realize from birth up until this present time that our brain records all events. It records what it sees, hears, tastes, feels and smells. Based on the interpretation from the brain, because of what it considers to be good or bad, it stores that data along with the event. All learned behavior. Suppose you had been complimented the majority of your life. You were told that you could do anything. You were told that you were more than a conqueror and that the earth realm was waiting on your contributions. You were wonderfully and marvelously made. You were separated from television, radio, the media of any kind, and away from people speaking negativity into your life. What do you think the outcome would be?

Look at it from the opposite perspective. Suppose you were told you are stupid and you will not amount to anything. You

♡ ***Tell the flesh, "you can only dig up things from my past; you do not know where I am going or how I will get there.***

were told you are ugly, you are clumsy, you are poor, and you are lazy and so on. Feed your mind with soap operas, reality shows, and surrounded by negative people. What images do you think are planted in this person? What do you think the outcome would be for this person if they did not have a drastic change in their life?

King David in Scripture stayed away from his family growing up the majority of the time. He was alone with nature and God tending to the family's sheep. The sheep could not tell David he would not be king. When Samuel came looking for one of Jesse's sons to anoint him, it does not seem any of the family thought it was David. David did not look like a king at this time, he did not dress like a king and he certainly did not smell like a king. But he had all the ingredients of a king inside him. David was confirmed and affirmed by His Heavenly Father who he conversed with quite often. David did not ask the outside world, people, media or even his flesh, "What do you think about me being king". David accepted his position, was anointed by Samuel, and then immediately went back tending to sheep and never doubted nor questioned that his kingship would come in due season.

Jesus spent quality time with his family and friends. But Jesus also spent a lot of time communing with His Father, God, establishing His relationship. At twelve Jesus was found in the temple answering questions and astonishing the leaders, but we really do not see Jesus out and about after that until eighteen years later. Jesus goes back into preparation, away from the world and those Pharisees and Sadducees types (modern day haters, those folks that want you to fail) before coming forth. He was established in who He was and why He was before He went out and mingled with the world who would try to convince him otherwise.

Why, because the world does not know. If He told the world God's purpose for Him, they would have tried to keep Him from accomplishing them. Sometimes you cannot reveal your dreams and visions to anyone! Shut your mouth and talk to God! Stop talking so much and listen to God, the one who knows!

The world has its own set of rules, its set way of doing things, and that is contrary to God's way. Perfect examples

♡ ***Stop talking so much and listen to God, the one who knows!***

are, God's word says to receive you give. The world says every man for himself, "I have, I keep and I strive to get more". God's word says we must love those whom despiteful use us; the world says you get them if they do something to you. God's word says love thy neighbor as yourself. The world says only love yourself; so you see why transforming your mind and becoming unattached to the world's way of thinking is so important for healthy spirits, minds and bodies.

All of us have been influenced by the world, you must go through reconstruction. All those negative images that have been written on your minds and hearts have to be rewritten. There has been someone or something that has created these negative images in your life.

Record something different on the tape
It is recorded on the tape recorder of your mind and it just keeps rewinding and replaying. What you have to do is go to God's Word find His Word for that situation, which is life, which is health and start writing over that part of the tape

until it has been completely rewritten to play what God says you are.

Growing up in a small town, there were things written on my tape that had to be rewritten. Growing up a black woman, there were things written on my tape that had to be rewritten. Anything that contradicts truth has to be rewritten.

And the tape gets written on daily. So you must guard your hearts with all diligence and be careful in what you take in through your ear gates and eye gates that end up on the tape recorder of your minds. Be careful as you rewrite the tape with God's words that they are guarded and kept intact. *Out of the heart flow the issues of life.*

We all have issues that are recorded on the tapes of our minds that keep us in fear, doubt, loneliness, depression and isolation that need to be rewritten.

Take God's word and keep rewriting over the tape, every time it comes up, you say what God's word says; "you are more than a conqueror. You can do all things through Christ Jesus and you are wonderfully and marvelously made". God did not give you a Spirit of fear, but of power, love and a sound mind. You were made in the image and likeness of

God. You are an over comer. Learn how to talk to the very heart of you.

> *In 1996 I started speaking confessions over my life and my family's life. I went to God's word, wrote His Word on over 200 index cards - all the things I could find about not having fear, and about being blessed in mind, body and spirit, and that God loved me. I kept referring to those index cards until that word became such a part of me, that I no longer needed the index cards, as I became the words. But now I search the scriptures for other WORD to use to apply to other areas as God reveals to me the parts of the tape that need to be rewritten on my heart. You are speaking positive reinforcement to your spirit.*

You know who you are, you are Spirit, and you know you have to rewrite the tape, so that your mind and emotions will line up according to who you are.

BODY

Now let's talk about the body. Even though it is only dirt, God did take the time to mold, shape and make these dirt suits. God thought it necessary for these bodies to be made to house the '*spirit*'. With that in mind you should value and appreciate your bodies but all done in perspective. Because your bodies are made from dirt, we know that eventually it will conk out and return back to the earth. Therefore, as long as you have been entrusted with these bodies you should take care of them.

How do you do that? First you should offer your bodies back to the Creator and ask for guidance and instruction. You should value them and care for them. You should not contaminate it with too much food, drink or anything. As soon as your body conks out, your Spirit no longer has any use for it (it gets up and out of there in a hurry).

Rest

There is a time and season for everything, including rest. We have become this society of people where everything is done quickly. All the appliances and things in our homes are made so we will have more time, but we never have time for anything. We are always running about, here and there, and a lot of time we are running around doing what we would call

God's work...But are we? Sometimes we get so busy doing God's work, that we stop consulting God and He's asked us to move on to something else years ago. We cannot do a Christian we have to be a Christian. It has to become your life your breath and who you are. You are not effective Christians if you are so busy doing it; you need to be it so the world can see Christ in you. This cannot be a Sunday ritual, but must become an everyday lifestyle.

Sleep and rest is essential, for the cells in your bodies to rejuvenate and to produce more healthy ones. God showed that rest was important because even He rested after His work, so who are you. You feel like you can get so much accomplished by pushing yourselves just a little harder to finish before stopping. The truth of the matter is normally it will have to be redone or reevaluated anyway. You were not at your best, so you are thinking more highly of yourself than you ought, because you think you are superwoman or superman (both fictional characters anyway), and you can juggle all these things, but you cannot successfully.

♡ **We cannot do a Christian we have to be a Christian. It has to become your life your breath and.**

Over a period of time of trying to fit too many things in a very small timeframe, brings about a feeling of being overwhelmed. God did not create all His work in one day so be mindful…do what you can, set goals and deadlines, take breaks, and get some sleep. Take away the stress and anxiety.

You have all these projects and you cannot do them all at one time, but you try and then you want to get stressed. Come on, there has to be balance. Your body is not a machine, even though some of you push your bodies harder than you would a machine. Take time to take a deep breath. Actually, take a deep breath, right now, and take another and another. Can you hear the quieting of your mind? That breath of life is God.

When there is chaos all around learn to stop, take a deep breath, realize God is right there with you. Deep breathing is also good for us, it has been proven that shallow breathing promotes stress and anxiety and the circulation of oxygen to

♡ **When there is chaos all around learn to stop, take a deep breath and realize God is right there with you.**

the brain is not as strong. (So breathing properly and correctly promotes circulation, heart regulation and clear mindedness).

We are a society that loves food. But we also like convenience, even if it cost us our health. Fast food is normally full of cholesterol, saturated fat, high in sodium, processed sugar, a lot of preservatives that we cannot pronounce, and steroids to produce the product a lot faster. We gobble it up, sometimes two or three meals a day and day after day. Some of you work late hours so you eat late at night. We are the keeper of the body so we need to treat them better. What you eat both spiritually and physically is important, so please read the labels carefully when doing so. You truly become a product of what you eat so the life you save just may be your own.

Cancer in a lot of cases can even be linked with diet. So if there are some things you can do yourselves to be proactive in maintaining healthy bodies – go ahead and do them. Why do you abuse your bodies to death, literally, by feeding it junk, but expecting it to perform perfectly?

When you buy cars, some of you change the oil every three or four thousand miles. You rotate the tires, you put on new brake pads, and you change bulbs when they go out. You wash the car, vacuum the car and put the car in the garage. You are doing all the proper maintenance functions to get the best potential or best performance from that car. Some of us treat our cars better than we treat our bodies. You have to be proactive where your bodies are concerned also; you need to have regular check-ups.

Where you have poor eating habits and addictions that are robbing your health you need to seek God for deliverance in any of these areas of your lives; (you can be delivered and set free from any strongholds because the Great Physician is Jesus). You need to do what you can to preserve the body; because you do not know how long you will need these earth suits.

When you mention the word exercise to some it is like you've cussed them. You may not be able to run the 50 yard dash, do TAE-BO or high-impact aerobics, but the majority of you can do some form of exercise. You could walk; lift your arms over your head while sitting. It is not what you do but the biggest results come out of doing some form of exercise and doing it consistently.

In God's Word you will notice that Jesus and the disciples walked almost everywhere, occasionally they took a boat ride, but even then they got a workout from rowing. You can even look at the diet of Jesus, which mostly consisted of honey, honey-comb, herbs, fish, milk, bread and water. Every now and then he did have lamb and some beef. Jesus' diet was little to no fat, low cholesterol, no preservatives, no processed sugar, and a no steroids. This diet is easy on the digestive system but high in nutrition.

We become so spiritually minded in some cases, we are no earthly good. Balance is the key to a successful life. Some of the poorest health conditions are among believers of Christ. We have not transformed our mind to include that God intended for all of "*you*" to be whole. Not just your spirit, but also the body that houses your Spirit and the mind that communicates to Spirit and body.

♡ ***Summary - Who are you; one may ask? What will you say? Look inside out before you answer. Will*** *you go before God? Will you say, "I want to be whole; I want to be complete in every area of my life".*

You are a spirit that is housed in a body and you have emotions or sensors that should be connected to your spirit that discerns between good and evil.

Your mind needs to be transformed so you can be made whole. You cannot change where you have come from, but starting from this moment forward you can help shape where you are going. You can feed your heart (spirit), mind and body with good stuff and as a result you can be better equipped to fulfill the purpose God has for you!

Key 1 notes:

Chapter 2
My Hidden Treasures

The kingdom of God is like treasure hidden in a field, Which a man found and hid; and for joy over it he goes and sells all that he has and buys that field.
~ Matthew 13:44

Why did you come to earth? What is your assignment? Have you stopped to ask yourself these questions? The whole course of our being here is about purpose and the Spirit of you will continue to seek that purpose in you until this journey.

One of the most tragic parts of dying is not death, but to die without knowing what you were ever sent here to do. Do you know how many dreams and ideas were buried with loved ones? Do you know how many cures to diseases and inventions we will never witness because people just like you and I did not take that chance on that idea?

I grew up in a two-parent family, with four older brothers and one younger sister. We grew up in a small rural town. My mother instilled my love for God. My father instilled hard work and persistence. I often think about how my parents and their parents and their parents before them where chosen so I would have just the right makeup for me to be me. When you reflect over your life (and some of us with more traumas and test than others), it is all purposed.

I cannot get hung up on being black and being a woman and that my ancestors came to America by way of a slave ship. I have to look for the deeper meaning and purpose why this is the way it is. Before I know what I am to do, I must know who I am. And before I can go somewhere I must recognize where I am currently and where I came from. You have discovered in the first chapter that you are Spirit, housed in a body and you possess a mind. Once you discover who you are then you can proceed to why you are created and why you are here in the earth realm.

Purpose calls you
You will not be fulfilled until you are doing what you were sent here to do. It does not matter how much money you

make or have made. It does not matter what status, fortune or recognition you have obtained.

If you are not walking in your called destiny, your purpose for being you, there is one thing that is true; there is still a longing in you to connect with this destiny. Your purpose calls you and you will not have that total peace until you are walking in its fullness.

I cried out to the Lord why did you send me here? This plea was not like any other plea I cried out before. This plea wasn't a cutesy plea, but one sincere out of a groaning from the heart. To discover your purpose for being here one must go to the source and the Creator who made you. Like purchasing a new car you are given a copy of the manufacturer's manual. Why? Just to be doing something? No, the manufacturer is the only one that knows the true intent or purpose of the product/thing they created.

♡ *If you are not walking in your called destiny, your purpose for being you, there is one thing that is true; there is still a longing in you to connect with this destiny.*

Let's say you purchased a new car, but you use the car as your house. You can live in your car and it may accommodate your sleeping needs, your reading, eating and many other activities you want to do in this so-called house of yours. Your house by way of your car has limited space, so you will never be able to walk around in your car.

You will never be able to take a shower in your car. Let's say the car sits in the same spot without being moved, because your car is your house and it is not being used as a car. Is the car being utilized to its' maximum potential being a house? If the car sits there without ever being driven what will happen? Well the battery will go weak. The tires will probably dry rot. All kinds of things could happen, because the car is not being cranked up to lubricate the oil through all the parts. Transportation was the full intent and purpose of this car. Every part put in the car was put in for this very intent. There was not one part put in by accident or one part put in that wasn't needed. All the parts have purpose to make the car complete. So the car being used as anything other than being a car is being misused or abnormally used (not utilizing something for the intent it was designed).

You may be working and it may be a successful career but if you are not fulfilling your purpose here on earth, you are not utilizing your maximum potential. There are some parts of you that are probably never utilized or tapped into.

I have a career in the computer technology field. The normal skill set for computer programmers are logic and analytical thinking. People normally think computer geeks are introverted and shy. As far as aptitude I would say I am an above average computer technologist and make a good living doing it, I am not driven to do it because it is not my passion. But I utilize the computer to help me research or use as a tool to help me in the thing I have a passion for – I will tell you later what this is. You should be doing that thing that causes you to lose all track of time, the thing you could do if money was not an object. On the other hand I cannot discard the characteristics and talents I have discovered as being in the computer technology field that may add to my purpose. For some reason God felt these traits were beneficial in my make up, so I cannot discard them.

Take five minutes and think of that something you do where you lose all track of time doing it.

Think of that something where if money were no object what is it you would be doing?

If you were able to answer both of these questions you are well on your way to discovering some key components of unlocking the hidden treasures deep inside you. Jot down in the notes area at the end of this chapter five things that you do well.

List five things professionally/personally that you would prefer not having to do. (These are things you do not particularly enjoy doing)

> If you are have trouble answering any of these questions it will help determine:
> 1. You do not have a good handle on what your personal gifts are
> 2. You could be in your chosen profession and therefore you do not see any limitations
> 3. You could be in your chosen profession and can be crossing over into some areas that are not a part of your purpose

You will need to start keeping a journal if you are not doing so or just getting a note pad and a pencil. Habakkuk 2:2 says, *"Write the vision and make it plain"*. Why do you need to write it down? Have you remembered everything that has ever entered your brain? I did not think so. When an architect or builder is designing a house or building, do you think they build a house from their heads? No it is pretty difficult to work from your head. There would be specifics you would leave out if you did not write it down.

You cannot visualize the completed building without it been laid out. Therefore a blueprint is necessary. This is also true for us to know what we are to do, we need a blueprint, and so every little detail that is given to you need to be recorded. It would be bad for a builder to have the blueprint completed but missed something like what size lot the house would be built on.

After my cry out to God I started writing everything down that came to me. God spoke to me with night dreams, daydreams, visions, His Spirit, through people and especially through His Word. I began spending a lot of time reading God's Word, reading a lot of other inspirational material, and listening to sermons like I was preparing for something ahead. After reading God's Word I was inspired to write from what I read. I have sticky notes and index cards all over the place. I was then inspired to record myself reading God's words. I didn't realize until later image was being formed from what I was reading and hearing. Romans 10:17 states, *"Faith comes by hearing, and hearing by the word of God"*.

Dreamer

I am a very colorful and detailed dreamer, but I admit I do not always get the correct interpretation before I am acting on the dream which is something I am learning more about each day, wait on God. The recording of dreams and visions will help you keep track if patterns are being formed in what you are dreaming as far as what God is saying to you.

I told you I would tell you what my passion is. I had a dream about a lecture room that I recognized to be a lecture room in the college I attended for undergraduate school. When I walked through the door to take a seat, I recognized my sister. She seemed agitated with me and she asked me "where have you been, we have been waiting on you to teach". I looked at her in fear as I asked, "teach what". She said you know, come on I will help you. I walked to the podium as she handed me index cards. As I looked down at these cards there were no words on them and I woke up. You sometimes may miss it trying to get it or you may go ahead of the appointed time, but that is okay, God will take those experiences and use them for your good.

I interpreted this dream to mean I would be teaching at my alma mater and I would be teaching computer technology because that is what I was doing at the time. I immediately got busy to walk in my calling. I called a girlfriend that worked at the college to inquire about any job openings. Guess what they did of course in the Business Information Technology Department. I posted for the job and got it. After two months there I say, Oh Lord, this cannot be my job. So thinking I was supposed to be there, I set out to get a master's degree hoping to move into a teaching position. I called the graduate school department, they were going to mail me the information. Time passed and when I thought about a master's degree again it is about three months later. I call them and they told me the graduate computer science school will not be accepting any more applications for the next three years, since it was the site for a visiting school's degree.

Well I go back to Father God, and whine about having to wait, three years to get into this graduate program. God answered with *"I did not tell you, you would be teaching computer science"*. Well now I am looking puzzled and feeling pretty crazy. This is what I have done for the last ten years what on earth then would I teach. He told me to go back and reevaluate the dream I had written down. There was a significant piece that I missed, I mean I flat out overlooked because it was so subtle. You recall me saying my sister handed me index cards and they had no words on them, they did not have words but they had pictures. Guess what the pictures where? They were all biblical characters; you know the pictures you may see in your Sunday school books (possibly meaning I would be teaching on spiritual or biblical principles).

Well I am no longer working at this college campus but I am still in the computer technology arena and I have moved into leadership positions and God continues to write the vision every day and make it plain. When you mess up, do not flip out, let God redirect your path and He will.

The opportunity came at my church for me to stand before people and start teaching bible study. Wow, I was scared to death, my knees knocked and my stomach felt like I was going to be sick, but after allowing the Holy Spirit to speak through me I died of Pam and I was edified by God speaking through me. I had tapped into something that left me feeling like I had tasted Heaven...Had I tapped into my passion...Had this teaching thing awakened my hidden treasure?

Very shortly after this door opened, God had my family to move to another church and I felt like I was on the Island of Patmos. I had made another assumption; I thought I knew where I would be doing this teaching. Do not assume anything with your purpose. Only assume I have one and the Holy Spirit knows what it is. After licking my wounds, crying and pouting, I realized the island was where I needed to be because the new church was an excellent teaching ministry and they had their own Bible College. *You cannot set boundaries or limitations on your purpose. It keeps unfolding and unfolding.*

I have since received a degree in Biblical Studies and a Certificate in Christian Leadership. I am completing a Doctorate Degree in Business Administration specializing in Leadership. And yes I am teaching at United Cornerstone School of Divinity with my husband (founder in 2005) who is the President.

God is speaking are we listening?

As I started to go back over all the scriptures that I had studied for the last 10 years, there were definite patterns formed. The majority of the scriptures I studied were of prophets speaking life to the people, telling them what God wanted to tell them to be free and liberated. (It is funny I really wasn't accustomed to reading a lot of the Old Testament. Now I love reading Jeremiah, Zechariah, Ezekiel, and Joshua; these men were all mouthpieces for God, so now the Biblical Studies degree is making sense as I'm teaching in a divinity school). God is amazing!

It is very important for you to keep pen and pad by your bed because if you wake up with the Holy Spirit speaking to you write it down. It may not make sense at the moment but it eventually will. It may be one word, three sentences, but please write it down. God will give you more and more as you are ready to handle it.

In 2005, I was reminded to go back to my journal and read entries from 1999. I found written on September 1, 1999, the Holy Spirit had spoken to me about teaching a dying generation about Jesus Christ. Pretty embarrassing to think six years had passed before I got the revelation but in 1999 I was not ready to understand spiritually what the dream meant. I still do not understand the dream to the fullest but I am definitely teaching, lecturing, motivating and moving in the direction in which my purpose is suggesting. I am definitely stepping out on faith with believing that God did put this in my heart and I have to do it or else.

Pure heart

I continued in 1999 to cry out to God again as I told God, "I hear you, where you lead I will follow, I do not know what, but if it is through my voice I will speak for you". I prayed for Him to put the Words in my mouth. Shortly after this, I woke up one morning with the word *"pure heart"* on my heart, so I wrote it down. A few months later I was given seven sentences so I wrote those down as well. I started praying life over "pure heart" and the seven sentences. As God revealed more to me, the seven sentences became seven lecture topics, and then the seven chapters to this book.

As things began to unravel God only showed me small bits, as He knows me. I will put the cart before the horse, and God has disciplined and is still working with me in this area. God gave me this great enthusiasm and zeal, but if it is not properly used it is just a ball of energy all in the wrong place, making a lot of noise but having no effect. I do not want that, so I am asking God each day to order my steps. You will need to pray for guidance and direction over everything because one wrong turn can have you in the wilderness for quite a long time.

Humility is a trait that you need to develop in a hurry in trying to discover purpose. You do not know what parts of your life or self you will be asked to share. Also the more God reveals to you, the more you become aware of how it is much bigger than you and you cannot do it without God. Keep this attitude, you cannot do it, but with Christ all things are possible.

♡ *Let's review some key points.*

1. *Discover who you are. Spend time each day paying attention to yourself. What are those things you just do naturally without thinking. What are those things you can do that you lose all track of time doing?*
2. *Know your Creator*
3. *What are those things you do that you prefer not doing? This tells you what are learned talents and skills versus God given gifts and talents.*
4. *Do proper research. Need to invest time in self. Study God's Word; spend quality time with your Creator seeking His will for your life.*
5. *Develop techniques to record or document vision. Keep a journal, carry a small tape recorder or just keep a small pad and pencil. As things are revealed to you through God's Word, through God, through dreams, through visions or through people record them.*
6. *Do not be afraid to act out on that unction that comes to you. Do not be afraid to try things. Do not be afraid to step out on faith, even when you get it*

wrong, at least you tried. There's a saying that goes, "I did not do it wrong this makes just 10,001 things I tried that did not work". After a while there is a process of elimination.
7. Realize the Spirit knows why He sent you, as you get closer to your purpose, He will speak clearer it will become real.

Key 2 notes:

Chapter 3
Pure Heart

Create in me a clean heart, Oh God, and renew the right Spirit within me

~ Psalms 51:10

Are you stuck in a rut spiritually? Do you feel there has got to be more to life than working every day, having a family and going to church on Sunday? Do you feel you are obviously missing something, and the part you're missing is the most crucial part?

I accepted Christ when I was thirteen years old on a Friday night at a Pentecostal Holiness church. I joined Oak Grove United Methodist Church where my mother was a member. I went to college, graduated from college, got a job, got married and had a child. We went to church every Sunday. Life seemed normal measured by man's standards. But guess what, life wasn't okay I was going through life on a treadmill. I was a "good" person by society's standards. But the reality that God lived in me just had not connected yet.

My mother was a spirit filled woman of God. She was an intercessor for the world and especially for her family. When trouble came my way I called her and went on my merry way. I knew my mother would be praying for me and she had a connection with God. So why should I lose sleep at night? But at some point in your life (some sooner than later) you will find out that you cannot reach God through your mother, your father or your grandmother. You have got to have your own relationship. When you call He answers on the other end. Every man, woman, boy and girl must have their own personal relationship with the Lord.

My father died in 1987 after a stroke and even though it was difficult, I had my momma to help me through this great loss. Who would have known that only two short years later my mother would be diagnosed with breast cancer? I hadn't reached thirty yet but I was sure I could cope with all life was sending my way. My mother went through surgery, treatments, radiation, and her prognosis was great. Eight months after her treatments my mother died, on September 11, 1990. I would have never guessed the impact this would have on my life other than just going through it. The later had become sooner and it was real.

The weeks following my mother's death were pure hell. I stopped going to church, I stopped reading my Bible and I stopped talking to God. I walked around angry with God, but I would not dare speak this verbally. I gave angry a new description and definition. I did not want to hear anyone saying oh, everything will be all right. I did not want anyone to say anything to me about what was going on with his or her mother. People absolutely got on my last nerve walking around grinning happy with those dumb smiles on their faces. I had a serious attitude and as a result I became bitter, angry and resentful even the more.

When you do not have your own personal relationship with Jesus, you selfishly look at the death of a loved one as a loss. Of course it was my loss I had lost a mother, a friend, a confident, a peace-maker, an encourager and especially a prayer warrior. Now what was I supposed to do? I had ran around all this time going to church, but did not realize I was the church.

My world as I knew it became colder, darker and more closed in. When I got a clue that something was desperately wrong I was in a psychiatric ward. I was taking antidepressants to cope during the day and downers to sleep at night. I just existed, living in a fog. This is a very vulnerable place to be in. Folks just giving you pills for your mind and emotions. You do not have the willpower, mind, or heart to do anything otherwise.

<u>Overcoming emotional and psychological bondage</u>

How can people effectively treat your mind and emotions? They cannot... there is no way you can do a sonogram and display emotions on a chart to treat them. I was so broken up, so depressed that I could not even reason, so hurt that pain become a way of life. It hurt so bad I really did not care who was making decisions for my life because everything was so muffled in my mind. I could not remember what day of the week it was. I could not remember if my mother really did die or if it was an ugly dream. I knew I had a daughter needing a mother to take care of her, but I could not even comb my own hair and did not even want to. I wanted everything and everybody to leave me alone so I could crawl up in my own little corner, in my own little chair and forget everything life had presented me.

I gave you some of my personal testimony to inform you that a bitter heart contaminates the mind and emotions. It will leave you in emotional and psychological bondage from which only a Savior and a Deliverer can free you. There are a lot of things that we let harbor in our hearts that will eat away at us just like the cancer that took my mother.

There are all kinds of strongholds that stifle us from moving forward. Some people were molested as children, and as a result you stored hatred in your heart. Some suffered physical, verbal or emotional abuse from being in abusive relationships. As a result you stored doubt in your heart. Some have been hurt because people that you loved and trusted just let you down or walked out on you. So you store up unforgiveness and loneliness. Some of you hurt because you feel life just has not been fair. So you may store up envy and jealousy. Some of you have suffered all kinds of sicknesses and diseases. You may have stored up bitterness. Others have suffered losses and traumas just like I did. So you could have stored up anger. Some of you have suffered from close friends lying on you. So you store revenge.

As you can tell the weights become heavier and heavier. As time goes on you do not even notice anymore that you are dragging around all of this baggage. This becomes your lifestyle. You have no joy, no peace, no happiness, no compassion, no love, no faith, because your heart is so contaminated. You are dragging around heavy weights of corruption. Your attitude towards life and others is negative and you complain about others needing to change failing to realize it is you that needs to change. Yes, I've been there!

Because of things that happen to us physically, we build up these walls spiritually. We vow to ourselves, that nothing or no one will ever hurt us again.

Not realizing that the walls we build in us for protection will keep people and stuff out, but they also keep us trapped behind the wall. We walk around truly defeated and frustrated because we do not know why we feel this way.

Something bigger than I

As the days passed while in the psychiatric ward something inside of me that was greater than the entire world and my circumstances started to rise up in me. I found myself encouraging, uplifting and speaking life and hope to the many others that were in this place. I remembered what my

♡ ***Not realizing that the walls we build in us for protection will keep people and stuff out, but they also keep us trapped behind the wall.***

mother and aunts had spoken over me as I encouraged these women. I realized the many impossible circumstances I had seen my mother and father successfully overcome. There were many women and teenagers in this place and I wondered why? My heart often goes out to that place and to the many people who will find themselves there. Help them Oh, God as you did me. Have mercy upon them.

I had gone many days without speaking. This behavior is a bit unusual since I love people and love to talk. One day I heard the cry from a certain lady as I sat quietly in group therapy that caught my attention. I couldn't take it one more day hearing the hopelessness and the pain. I stood to my feet and said; stop it, just stop it, what nonsense is this? You come in here day after day, speaking about your pain and hurt and think you are going to leave feeling better. How you figure? I begin to speak life and everything I had been taught about the love of God came flooding to the forefront. I went to my room after this feeling better than I had in a while.

Women started to visit my room on a continuous basis. I had so many visits in the days to come until it was hard to distinguish who was the psychiatrist and who was the patient. I remember getting called to the front desk asking me to go visit the psychiatrist. After counseling sessions, evaluations, prescriptions and plenty of drugs the psychiatrist released me. The psychiatrist told me they could not find anything wrong with me other than exhaustion and grieving the loss of my mother and they needed to release me because my "spiritual" counseling sessions were interfering with their "psychological" counseling. It's ironic because he did ask me if I had considered going into counseling.

Wow, so when they sent me home there was one emotion raging after another. I was afraid of leaving the hospital because of what I had to face at home. Where were all these feelings coming from? Definitely, from inside me! It was coming from the walls of my heart. They had been written one by one, line upon line, year upon year, experience upon experience, and conversation upon conversation.

God wants to tell you something

After going home I had this great idea about getting away for a few days. I worked for the airlines so we could fly with no problems. So off to the Bahamas we go and I am uptight about everything. Yes, the Bahamas are beautiful and I had enjoyed it in previous visits, but this particular trip everything just looked unimpressive. One morning as I was leaving the hotel a lady came from out of nowhere and grabbed me by the arm. I told her to get her hands off of me and I did not have any money to give her. She said, "*God wants me to tell you something*". Yes sure I am thinking, she wants some money. In her native Bahamian dialect she began by saying "*God knows you are angry with Him, but He still wants to talk to you*". I looked around like *she ain't talking to me*. She continued by saying, "*you are mad because you lost your mother*". As the tears rolled down my face I am immediately slapped back into this planet. She said, "*God wants to talk to you because He loves you*". Oh my God, He loves me, He loves me and somewhere I must have thought He hated me because he took away the people that loved me. Do you realize love heals all hurts? I had never considered this before this time that God loved me more than my mother or father ever could.

When I truly looked at myself I had to confess with my mouth and repent, God I am angry with you. You took my parents and I am mad! We must admit to God how we truly feel. Guess what He knows anyway. Only a *'pure heart'* knows what is true. We want to dress it up, cover it up and live a life of fake and pretense...but the person that really suffers is you. Be true to thine self.

God's answer was *"I came that you might have life and have it more abundantly"*. I did not understand His answer just yet. How could taking my parents have anything to do with abundance it felt like loss to me? I would have to get back with Him, when I decided to talk to Him again, and this was not that day.

As the days went by it seemed not only were my emotions everywhere, so was my physical body. I had not been feeling well for months so I went to the doctor and they tested me for diabetes. They did not find anything wrong with me. About three weeks later I was in the emergency room where I was showing all the symptoms of a massive heart attack. After every test possible the physician told me I had lungs and arteries as clear as a bell and should live to see 100; but what was going on?

♡ ***We must admit to God how we truly feel, guess what He knows anyway. Only a 'pure heart' knows what is true.***

Well they couldn't find anything physically wrong with me but I must tell you, I was an emotional mess.

You should be aware that your psyche can get so off balance that it can bring on physical illnesses or have your mind mimicking illnesses, such as mine did. This comes from all the bad images in your heart that plays over and over in your mind that I mentioned in a previous chapter. I must add that these symptoms were not just flaky symptoms, they revealed other things written on my heart. Diabetes was an illness that is in my family history, so my mind was trying to claim this generational curse. Breast cancer was another illness that was in my family history so you can become guilty of saying, "this disease or illness is in my family". Sometimes even attaching the fear with it, which is saying most likely I will develop such and such.

We say religiously, Lord create in me a clean heart and renew the right spirit within me. We should say this with conviction and truth. A contaminated heart will kill you physically, mentally and spiritually. Only God knows all the junk that we have written in our hearts and minds. If you don't deal with it at some point, later in your lives you will not have a choice.

Being made whole

As my healing process started to take place, I began like never before reading the word of God. I listened to worship and easy listening music. I watched happy shows and programs that made me laugh. I connected back with nature and reintroduced walking, exercising and taking deep breaths again.

I asked God again, "why did you take my momma"? He answered, *"The thief comes to kill, steal and destroy, I came that you might have life and have it more abundantly, and I want you whole"*. I started to cry with much repentance as I asked God how could I be made whole. He said give me all those things in your heart that are not pure. I repeated it *"give you all the things in my heart that are not pure"*. God answered yes, have *clean hands* and a *pure heart*.

You know you have heard people say, "then instantly I was healed". It did not happen that way for me. I did a lot of crying and a lot of praying. Somewhere in the course of the next nine to twelve months I no longer looked for the antidepressants or the sleeping pills, thank God. God gave me a treatment for purifying the heart and it is still being administered. I needed time to talk to God so He could reveal to me all the impurities in my heart that I needed to get rid of and only He could help to remove them.

Surgery from the Great Physician

When I had the symptoms of the heart attack in the physical God revealed to me later that there was surgery needed to take place in the spiritual realm for my spiritual heart. I truly had suffered a heart attack in my spiritual heart as it was truly clogged up with no open arteries leading to the life source of Jesus Christ. John 15:15 says, *"I am the vine and you are the branches"*. I was in bad shape. In my case I needed a quadruple bypass in the spiritual heart, and only the Master Surgeon could perform such a procedure, and that is Jesus.

The best part about this Surgeon is He can remove the ailment by cutting it with a two-edged sword of His Word; treat the illness at the root, seal you back up with the Holy Spirit without stitches or scars. Pretty amazing, humph!

I had about a thirty-five minute commute to work, and my daily routine would be to listen to gospel music. I had made a plea earlier to God wanting more time to spend with Him. Something happened to the mechanics of the stereo system in my car, so I had to ride to and from work in silence. Be careful when you make a plea you just may have to adhere to it.

Do you realize how accustomed some of you are to noise? If some of you do not have a lot of noise going on around you, you cannot function. How can you hear from God with all the external noise, shut it off and listen to the still and quiet voice that is within you?

After about the fourth day I could not wait to drive to and from work, I would sit in the parking lot for another fifteen minutes after I got to work just to complete my talk with God. God wanted to talk to me and I finally had time with no distractions or disturbances and He had much to say. God told me *"the truth would make you free"*. God also told me *"cancer is not of me; sickness, and evil are in this world because of sin. But my Son, Jesus the Christ, came to earth and paid the ultimate price to overcome sickness, death, and the grave"*. God also revealed to me that being made whole involved more than a physical healing but that all three parts of me would need to go through a transformation. And realizing the biggest transformation must begin in the mind. God also wanted me to know there were some things I need to do.

<u>Not my soap operas</u>
God revealed to me that He wanted me to give Him another two hours that He had found in my day. Well I did not see any extra time, but God showed me I would record the soap operas and after I had cooked dinner, washed the dishes, got my daughter situated and before going to bed I would relax with the soaps for exactly about two hours. Amazing, again, chuckle!

God revealed to me I was contaminating my heart with more junk. I was spending about 70 minutes in prayer each day with my commute to work. But listened to the world around me anywhere from eight to ten hours at work and then topped it off with two hours of soaps and expected to have a pure heart. How do you figure? It is not deep, what goes in is exactly what you are going to get out?

After much conviction and repentance I gave God the two hours that I had used for soaps to study His word, pray and meditate.

As time passed and a more intimate fellowship with God developed, I was amazed that I had functioned as well as I had with all that was wrong with me. My heart was so contaminated with fear, doubt, hate, bitterness, prejudices, jealousy, envy, pride, selfishness, unforgiveness, vanity, thinking at some points too low of myself and others too high, lust of the flesh, and the hardest was trying to be a perfectionist. Let me clarify here being a perfectionist is different than working in excellence which I like to do but there is only one perfect and that is Christ.

As God begins to reveal to you, those impurities in your heart, ask Him to help you deal with them and remove them. Warning! You cannot remove them yourself. These are things that have been there in a lot of cases since you were infants or very small children and they have some pretty deep roots. Some of these are things you are not even aware of at this time.

You have to get the word of God that applies to that situation; speak life to that area, consistently, persistently and boldly.

As God begins to reveal to you, those impurities in your heart, ask Him to help you deal with them and remove them.

How do I seek a pure heart?

1. **You have to talk to God. You have to spend quality time with God your Creator to find out what is of Him and what is not.**
2. **When things are revealed to you from God (and they will be) admit it, do not deceive yourself and say that is not me. You want to be whole and the sooner you can admit and confess all of this junk the sooner your healing is on the way.**
3. **Once the issue is revealed ask God to heal you and what do you do next.**

Going through the process

Depression was a generational curse on the maternal side of my family. My mother suffered from it, some of her sisters and I am pretty sure her mother and on and on. A lot of these things that are in our hearts just did not show up with the experiences we are in, but they were passed down just like the family china.

The word in 1 Timothy Chapter 7; *"God did not give me a spirit of fear, but of power, love and a sound mind"*. I have a sound mind. I have to remind myself of this even today, Pam you have a sound mind. Your emotions are stable; you are healthy, well and whole.

Something else you need to prepare yourself for, when you go to God sincerely wanting Him to release you of all the junk that is in your heart the only person He deals with is you. I would go to God and pray; God you see this going on, fix this person or that person. God change my husband, my friend, or my co-worker. God would say, Pam I need you to start seeing this situation through my eyes. Pam you need to love more. Pam you need to forgive. Do not keep track of the number of things you feel that has been done to you. Forgive them all and I mean everyone. My response would be; God you do not understand, they did this to me, and your word says do not mess with your children. Like He really didn't understand.

Well I want you to know this is not easy, at least it was not for me. If I have to go before God and repent and cry I wanted everyone else to go before God and get there little whippings also. But the more you go before God, the more you do want to come with a pure heart.

Before going to the next chapter if there are areas in your life that you need help in… write them down and pray to the Father to help you. He will. Do you have some people you need to forgive? If your answer is yes, make a vow that you will go before the Lord every day for Him to help you forgive these individuals and forgive yourself for holding them in bondage? Keep doing this until you have forgiven them and you are free. Every time this person comes to your mind, say you are forgiven, I forgive you and I release you. Sometimes we cannot move forward because we are being held captive in unforgiveness.

It is important that we guard our heart with all diligence. Be mindful of the television shows you watch.

I have been discussing getting the junk out of our hearts, but I need to focus a little on what to put in our hearts after the junk is removed. Philippians 4:8 states, *"Finally, brethren, whatsoever things are true, whatsoever things are honest, whatsoever things are just, whatsoever things are pure, whatsoever things are lovely, whatsoever things are of good report; if there be any virtue, and if there be any praise, think on these things"*. These are things to write on your heart. There is so much negative stuff in the world, all around us; you will need some good stuff in your heart that you will be able to rely on in days to come.

If you read the newspaper or watch the news, wow! If it were rated it would be rated 'R'. You can be feeling like you are more than a conqueror, then listen to thirty minutes of news and it will counteract the positive. This person was shot, this person was raped, this person was attacked, and this person was stabbed, is what you hear blaring from your television. These are not good images to plant in your heart before you go to sleep. Read God's word and meditate on it day and night. Let the last thing your eyelids see before shutting them for sleep is God's word.

I have to be careful and I am serious when I say this about looking at the news on television or reading the newspaper. I cannot tell any of you to stop reading the newspaper or watching the news, but be careful in what you hear and what you write on your heart. You must realize the media is controlled by the world's system in doing things. That is why they want to give you the most violent, filth, vulgar, and disgusting stories they can give you in ten minutes. They want to capture you in the first few minutes to have your interest. Have you ever noticed they come out stating " to find out who robbed and killed such and such stayed tuned in it is coming up in the next segment'? They keep you tuned in and the most publicized story is last as they feed your heart with each explicit detail. They would have had you taking in all of their media for the entire segment. The media is a very influencing forum, be careful of what you hear. That is why it is called tel-e-vision because it is telling a vision. Just make sure it is aligned with your vision.

The eye gates and the ear gates are the two portals where most of the negative images enter your heart. Stuff that you saw in your childhood or heard in your childhood that formed an image of something that was not pure was written on your heart. It continues as adults. You take these images in through the senses. You should be warned what you have received, perceived, and even had stamped on your heart just may not be truth.

♡ *Wanting a pure heart must start with you, and receiving a pure heart must end with God.*

Key 3 notes:

Chapter 4
Love the Center of my Joy

Love never fails.
~ *1 Corinthians 13:8*

What is love?

We all think we have known love to some degree, so let's try to identify some of the characteristics and attributes that make up love. Could we say that love is an action word? That to love one must demonstrate some action.

John 3:16, says, *"For God so loved the world that He gave His only begotten son, that whoever believes in Him should not perish but have everlasting life"*. God demonstrated the first act of love toward us. He loved us so much He gave. Action took place in this case and God did not give us something He did not want, but He gave His most prized possession, His only son because He loved us. Love, pure love, genuine love, and unconditional love causes you to want to demonstrate your best toward the person(s) you love. You do not want to hold back anything, but you want the person you love to know how you feel about them because you were/are in LOVE. You want to spend time with this person. You could spend hours talking with this person on the phone. You want to do something for this person to let them know how you feel.

Then the clock strikes twelve and Cinderella is not a beautiful princess anymore and your Prince Charming turns back into the frog on the lily pad. How do you handle it when all those dreams have turned back into rags and you were left with one shoe, but it wasn't a glass slipper.

This can happen in dating, in marriage and in any relationship. You know why? We are all good at fronting. You know what fronting is? That is showing a person just one side of you... the good side. Fronting is just that, a front. You are nothing like the person you show to people. The bad, ugly and the different comes out much later when you feel like you no longer have to work at this relationship because I am already in there.

Do you know what you are looking for in a love relationship? Do you realize that we even learn behavior and attributes that we say are love? Does it sooth the emotions?

Does it feed the physical? What about your *'spirit'*? We are three parts and if any part is not whole then we are not complete. Do you realize that we all have baggage? What baggage, you ask?

Love is something we look for even at birth. We want to be soothed, cooed, provided for and feel like we are so special to some person.

Child Psychiatrist Gail Fernandez described a Reactive Attachment Disorder (RAD) in adults and children, that is linked to an infant not being held, therefore the infant never properly bonds to anyone[1]. This results in an overwhelming since of behavioral problems in older children and/or adults, because they do not know how to properly express feelings inside them to another person. They also have problems trusting people and build up walls to protect themselves from being hurt.

♡ *Love is something we look for even at birth we want to be soothed, cooed, provided for and feel like we are so special to some person.*

---

[1] Fernandez, Gail, MD., *"Reactive Attachment Disorder"*, Child Development Institute LLC, 1999

The two different types of behavior that have been noted that can occur if children have suffered these trauma. Some behaviors show that the child or adult will latch on to any and every one that show them some attention. The other behavior is totally opposite in nature where the child or adult will never trust anyone to get close because they feel they will be abandoned.

So here we are growing up in all kinds of environments. So called love could have been expressed to you by incest. It could have been expressed by physical and/or verbal abuse. We could have been victims of parents physically and verbally abusing one another, therefore those seeds and images are planted in our heart as well.

My father was a weekend alcoholic. I really did not see my father express any affection toward my mother. Not because he did not love her, but because he did not know how. He never saw it expressed when he was growing up. You see where I am going. Young men learn from their fathers or lack thereof. Young girls learn from mothers or other female images in their lives. If you let the television be your children's role model or what you look for in relationships, realize they are packing their bags with all the stuff they see and hear. We all have baggage and at some point in a relationship your dirty laundry will come out and so will the other person's whom we are in relationship with.

A bitter heart contaminates the mind and emotions. You could end up in such emotional and psychological bondage that only a Savior and a Deliverer can help you; take it from someone who knows. There are a lot of things that we can let harbor in our hearts that will eat away at us and we do not love anyone including ourselves as a result.

Have you ever been in a relationship where the love went sour? This thing described earlier as beautiful, wonderful and exciting that caused you to not only look stupid but to

♡ ***A bitter heart contaminates the mind and emotions***

also do stupid things, could go sour? How is that? Love is pure, love is unconditional, and love is genuine right. So what happened? Love is action and we just do it, it does not require all these things that the other person has to do to us or for us, for us to love. We cannot hold them ransom. We either love them or not with no strings attached.

A famous singer recorded a song a while back entitled, "*What does love have to do with it*"? I am sure you are reading this now asking the same question. What does love have to do with it?

There is a natural calling inside of us for love. We are created in the image and likeness of God and He is love.

God is the only person both the noun and the verb "love" applies to because God is love and God loves. I have heard people say, no one has ever loved me. Well if you have never known something how can you measure when you have it or not. The reason no one can say no one has loved me is because inside all of us is the natural love of God. What you are trying to say is there has not been a person in my life experience that has demonstrated the attributes that this center of me is seeking.

Scars are just reminders

I remember a time in my life when I felt so all alone, sad and unloved. While growing up I knew both my parents loved me, that my brothers and sisters loved me. I knew my relatives and friends loved me, but I was longing for something else. I had married and thought this was love. I met this man as a teenager while I was still in high school. We became friends and married when I graduated from college. We were on a fast track to success and on our way to the cover of Ebony Magazine and then you have to face reality. I never thought it could happen to me. Drugs are a demon from the pit of HELL with the sole purpose not only to destroy the addict, but those in their life as well. (This was an ordeal I do not wish upon anyone but I cannot get sidetracked here, that's another book within itself). You can have expectations from individuals that they can never deliver. We come to relationships broken ourselves and expecting other broken individuals to complete us.

Going through a divorce was like experiencing the loss of a loved one that I am all too familiar with. I never thought I would have that experience. It left me feeling like I was contaminated and that I walked around wearing the scarlet letter "*D*" stamped on my forehead. I felt everyone that looked upon me considered me a failure. How could I ever minister to anyone else after this ordeal? But what I failed to realize and count on was the love of God. God loves me. Yes even today, all day, every day God loves me.

So until I connected with God's love there was a void in me that no one could fill. And something in me needed something more. It wasn't something I could buy. It wasn't something I could eat or take a pill for. I had a longing, a yearning for something and I hadn't found it yet.

He loves me

I became a Christian when I was thirteen, I grew up in the church and I had accepted Christ. But when I was as low as I could go and tears were flowing down my face for no reason, then what? When I wanted to give up and throw in the towel and say this life is just too hard, then what? While I was feeling down and depressed for all the mistakes I had made, then what? The shame and guilt of my past had robbed me of hope and belief. When I had fallen and I couldn't get up, I heard someone knock on the doorway of my heart. I heard a quiet voice, saying *"Pam, let me come in"*.

I said *I hear you, I cannot see you, and I am just too broken to let anyone in.* Oh, "I heard that quiet voice say, *you do not have to do any work, just invite me in and I will do the rest".*

I said *Jesus* and before I could finish His name, He had walked right through the guilt, the shame, the pain, the hurt, the brokenness, the filth and the stench and said I want to live here. *I had accepted Christ as my Savior with my head but I did not invite Him to live in my heart. There is a difference!*

Do you know what that feels like? Allow the three that are one to live right inside you. You talk about fireworks! What a celebration took place inside of me, right there in my heart. What does love have to do with it? Where do I start? It has everything to do with it. Without Him loving you, you can never know what love is. I never knew of a love that could be so pure, so real, just for me. And He loves me just the way I am! I do not have to pretend to be something I am not. I do not have to buy Him stuff to try to win Him over. I do not have to make excuses for being born a woman. I do not have to apologize for being born African American. I do not have to fit in this group or that clique. He adores me, just the way I am. Without experiencing this real genuine love, you can never experience real joy!

What's the purpose for this love and this joy? Glad you asked.

The story of Joy

I heard this story a few years back and it expressed love, joy, laughter, pure heart, the Spirit of God, and I can, I will, and I must in such a beautiful way. There was a lady I will call Joy. Joy was in her 70s and lived with one of her 2 adult children. Joy enjoyed life, her grandchildren and she made a point to laugh and love a lot. Joy's children did not understand why she did not act like most grandmothers and ladies her age. She was always rolling around on the ground with her grandchildren and chasing her grandchildren around the house. Her children thought this was outrageous. She needed to act like a grandmother and not like the grandchildren's playmate. So Joy wanting not to ruffle any feathers decided to go to the psychologist that the children had referred her to. Joy was not fitting the mold that society had dictated so she must by crazy.

As the story continues, the psychologist lets you know up front, he wasn't there to help Joy, but she had been sent there to help him. When he first met Joy he notices numbers tattooed on her right wrist. He thought that this grandmother was going through some growing old syndrome and she possibly did not have a normal childhood but had some things to go on during her mid-life so now she must be acting out some of those whims. He asked Joy how long she had the tattoo on her wrist? A smile came to her face as she shares, sometimes she forgets the tattoo, but every time she is reminded of the tattoo she is filled with peace.

She shared with the doctor how she had been taken as a prisoner in a Nazi camp when she was a young girl. A method that the Nazi's used was to brand them with their own personal numbers so they could keep track of them. She shared of her experiences in the camp. She was given two biscuits a day and water for a meal, one in the morning and one in the afternoon. She talked about the sad cries and pleas she heard spill out of that camp. She shared how night seemed not only to bring out the saddest cries but the darkest and most dismal feelings. She mentioned how something greater than her talked with her inner most being and told her she would survive this.

Joy became the hope and the sunshine of the camp. She started getting up early in the morning and went to visit all the sick in the prison camp. She spoke of life and hope to them. After a while the word got around that she could make you feel better by her just talking to you and people waited every day for her visits.

One morning Joy woke up feeling down, depressed and so alone. As she started walking that voice spoke to Joy again and told her to walk everyday around the entire prison camp and for her to envision that she was on the outside walking. This particular day, outside of the gate Joy saw a dog that was so skinny. She still had part of her biscuit tucked away in a pocket for later; she shared it with the dog. Every day Joy took that walk she found the dog was outside of the gate waiting to greet her. She became aware in her heart that prison had nothing to do with the walls around her, but how she would deal with everything from this day forth. So she purposed in her own heart, that she was free.

As time passed many months and years later, she was able to walk free from that prison camp. But deep inside of Joy she had walked free from that prison camp many months prior. Joy had learned of a love so great in that prison camp that soothed her to sleep at night. This love wiped every tear from her face as she lay on her cot. This love nourished each biscuit with enough nutrients that Joy remained healthy while living in these conditions. This love kept her mind and emotions at peace even when the army soldiers yelled and mishandled her.

When she looked at the tattoo of numbers on her wrist she was reminded of that place. She said I did not want them removed because every time I look at them I am reminded of a LOVE so real that He will never leave you or forsake you. Even when no one else is around, He will send you companionship like he did me a little skinny dog, just to let me know, I do care and I am right here. Joy said, "I know my children think I am crazy, because I live each day just like it is my last". But I will continue to laugh big and I will love big, because Love Himself loved me big.

This story has stuck with me because it reminded me of a place I walked from physically and thank God was able to also walk free from mentally. Once you have been touched by Love Himself you cannot remain the same nor do you want to. Love is so pure He will reveal to you every issue about you. Love will reveal all those people you hate and have prejudices against just so He can help remove it. So for all those people who annoy you and all those people you just cannot get along with, He's speaking to something that is inside of you and your mirror attract that's not so pleasant a characteristic because it is in you. And He will keep bringing it to your attention until it is dealt with.

When you look around you will see someone that does not look like you. What have you been taught about them? Are they too big, too small, too white, too black, too brown, too woman, too man, too rich, too poor, too dumb, too intelligent? We all have prejudices and yes they are learned just like all the other stuff that is stored up there in our brains and hearts. But as long as I do not like you or won't love you for you, is the very thing that will keep me from truly achieving all that God has sent me here to do. You can hold the very key to my destiny, but if I walk around hating you because of your gender, your race, your economic status, guess who will miss out. We both would, I need you and you need me. God wants us to deposit in the earth all He has blessed us with so it will be used by the whole. Prejudice is something a lot of people like to avoid or dance around. But let's face this giant once and for all.

Where do prejudices come from? Would you say a lot of them come from a lack of knowledge? Some come from fear. Some come from people wanting to feel important so they have to belittle you so they can feel superior. Why do I need to feel superior? My point is, each time you answer one question it automatically causes another question to be formed. All of these prejudices and fears come from not knowing the truth. The truth will make you free.

How can I get this freedom? First of all you have to accept this love that is freely offered you. When you do not love yourself you cannot love someone else. Abused people abuse people. When the Pharisees asked Jesus which is the greatest commandment in the Law, Jesus replied in Matthew 22:37-40: *"'Love the Lord your God with all your heart and with all your soul and with all your mind', This is the first and greatest commandment. And the second is like it: Love your neighbor as yourself".* It took me a while to get the understanding of this Scripture but it is saying learn to love God who is love first with all three parts of you. Once you learn how to love from Love then you can love others. And if you love others the way God intended there isn't need for all the other commandments because you would not be doing anything to anyone to bring them hurt, harm or pain.

But to get this love you must accept love that is unconditional with no strings attached because it has been paid for in full. To accept this love requires a much deeper revelation to sink in rather than you just getting goose bumps. Almost a year God had me to go over the same thing. Pam before I can show you this, you must understand the depths and the widths of my LOVE. I thought I knew Jesus loved me. But I did not know that Jesus really loved me like that. What do I mean? I mean I had to experience His love with my heart instead of my head.

There is a part to us that truly does want to please God. You feel as though you will never get there. The harder you try to do it right, to be nice; to go that extra mile is the same time you keep on messing up. So you become frustrated with yourself. But keep on trying.

I am hard on me. I see I cannot do it alone. This is the love that God was trying to teach me. Pam stop trying to be a perfectionist...It is not by works, not by your efforts, but because of my love and my love alone is why I died on a cross, just for you. Can you just let go and let God love you?

Can you let Him love you because He's God and He chooses to love you just the way you are? Will you let Him love you right where you are? Will you let him love you so much that every tear you have shed He collects them to refresh you with later. Every stumble you will make He is right there to clean and wipe the wound and put His band-aide of love on it and kiss the boo-boo. Yes God loves you.

Key 4 notes:

Chapter 5
Laughter for the Soul

A merry heart makes a cheerful countenance

~ Proverbs 15:13

Take a deep breath... Breath is our connection to God and when we are feeling overwhelmed we need to be anchored with our strength and source.

I must warn you, you may laugh in this chapter. If this will offend you, go against your religious beliefs, or is not appropriate for your race, gender or age; you have permission to stop laughing anytime you get ready. I would not advise you to stop laughing because does a body good.

Have you ever laughed so hard that you cried, that your head hurt, that your nose was running and you had snot everywhere? Have you ever cried so hard you thought your heart would break and you possibly could not have any more tears? You really thought that you were dying I mean right then. Then after you stopped crying you really did break out and start laughing.

Yes we all have, but guess what, you are reading this book, which tells me, God's grace was sufficient and you made it through the bad times.

When I was given this chapter, I thought, God now what am I supposed to write about? Should I list some funny jokes. I heard God say with His sense of humor, *as funny as that would be Pam you are not a comedian so stick to the gifts I gave you.* I want you to stick to speaking on love, joy, peace, happiness and laughter. I said, "God how can I speak laughter in someone's life?" He said, "The way you speak healing, the way you speak blessings, the way you speak kindness all with my words. If you want laughter you must sow seeds of laughter".

We never stop to think that God's word could be filled with laughter, but it is just as it sings music to our soul. Some of us seem to think that God does not smile or laugh! We think He sits in Heaven with a prune face waiting to zap us. I want you to know this is definitely a wrong image of our Father God. God wants us to smile, laugh, and be filled with joy. That is why He tells us to be anxious for nothing. He also tells us in Jeremiah 29:11, *"He knows the thoughts that*

He thinks toward us and it is good and not of evil". Well if you have nothing to worry about or to fret over, that is worth laughing about right?

As I was preparing this chapter, I thought about some specific scriptures that I have read that have actually put a smile on my face with comfort, but also candidly showed our human nature of insecurities and how the world views Christians in a lot of cases.

Laugh at your fear

One scripture that comes to mind is "After Jesus had fed the multitude of five thousand He asked his disciples to go ahead in the boat before Him to the other side of the Sea of Galilee near Capernaum and He would catch up with them later. Jesus had gone up to pray and He could look out over the ocean and see the disciples rowing with difficulty and fighting against the winds". Picture this... The disciples are out in a boat around dusk in the middle of a body of water when they spot a figure walking on the water. The scripture says that Jesus would have walked right by them, but the

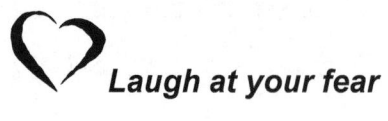

Laugh at your fear

disciples are scared out of their minds. These are the guys that are with Jesus day in and day out and they have seen Jesus perform miracle after miracle. But they see something walking on the water and they immediately think it is a ghost.

Admit it, when you read this you get a little tickled, because this sounds just like us. Fear can make us look really silly. Jesus had to tell them, "Do not be afraid, it is just me". So when the scriptures show you how even God's elite and the chosen ones still had doubt, fear and looked pretty silly at times, it was to assure us we aren't alone. This is how we look when storms come in our life we too are screaming and yelling... Help! We fail to see Jesus walking right there beside us, but we can count on Him. He is always there to reassure us do not be afraid and He will get right in the boat with us. Go ahead and laugh at yourself and get over it. You have been in this position of fear long enough…whatever ghosts are keeping you from getting to the other side you need to address them and ask God to help you overcome them.

Another humorous incident is found in the book of Acts chapter 2 the Day of Pentecost when the Holy Spirit manifested Himself among God's people. It was truly a Holy Ghost experience and a party like no other. Everyone there was intoxicated in the Holy Spirit, pretty dazed and speaking in different languages. The locals and the town folks are looking at the church folks and saying what are those "Holy Rollers" doing now. They are down here in the middle of the street drunk and talking out of their heads early in the morning. Well they were not drunk with alcohol and the world did not know what was going on with them. So we can look pretty funny and comical to the world and even other believers. Do not let this bother you, 1 Corinthians 1:27 says, "*God chose the foolish things of the world to confound the wise*".

When I was growing up my mother was a worshiper. When the Holy Spirit moved in her she would get a bit vocal so I would look around to see who was looking at us. Other children would be pointing their fingers, hunching one another, and chuckling at her display of praise. I would slouch down in the pew, desperately wanting my mother to sit down and act the way a "church mother" was supposed to act in church. No one else's mother was dancing around the place. You see I grew up in the United Methodist denomination, okay. And this behavior was embarrassing to me., because society has even dictated how churches should worship our God. So many of us were held and still are in bondage to denominations and how we should "act" in church. But the things that look so silly and foolish may be the very things you need to be doing for your breakthrough. So you need to ask God to help you unlearn all the things of the world that would keep you in bondage and that includes the shackles on laughter.

Laughing about our experiences brings healing
As an adult I laugh at these experiences now because after growing up leaving home, marrying, and having a child the seats change. Surviving a little drama, trauma, and tragedy in your life it can introduce radical worship to your life. I thank God that my mother passed down that David worship Spirit to me and I know there have been times I have looked and will look completely hilarious. When I praise the Lord I lose my jewelry, hats, scarves and cannot remember where I was sitting. My mascara will be running down my face but I do not care who's looking or what they are saying either (because if you have been where I have been looking crazy for Jesus is a minuscule thing). Just totally messed up!

My daughter would sometimes reach up to stroke my hand or she would give me the signals, please sit down momma. She does not know what's in store for her one day, she'll be having a momma performance. We pass down everything else why can't our legacy be passing down a genuine experience of worship!

Sometimes at home when things are really chaotic in my life, I turn my stereo up full blast to Fred Hammond or Kurt Franklin and praise the Lord just like I am losing my mind right there in my den. When I finish I feel better, by just standing up, crying, laughing and dancing.

Some of you need to tap back into the child that is in you. Some of you are just too stiff, some are just too proper, some are just too reserved; some are just so concerned about what people around you are saying. Some of us need to learn how to stick our chest out and throw our head back and laugh, laugh, laugh until you cry.

Ha, Ha, on your problems. Ha, Ha, on the bills are due. Ha, Ha my husband left me yesterday. Ha, Ha on that job. Ha,

Ha, one thing after the other. You may say Pam you just do not understand. Let me ask you this, did crying change one thing about your situation? I am the first to admit it comes natural for women to cry. The crying has its purpose in relieving some stress. But to continue to wallow in the mess, does not help, God only honors His Word. Laugh at the problems, laugh at the mountain and say, "be thou removed and cast into the sea".

King David tells us in the 23rd Psalm, "Yea thou I walk through the valley of the shadow of death, I will fear no evil". He is telling us here, I want to die because I feel like I am in the pits of Hell, but I will not focus on the pit nor Hell, because I am walking through…I am coming out on the other side. David realized he was not walking alone, he realized it was all about determination and a made up mind. He realized I can lay down and die right here or I can keep going to see where the end is going to be! The end for him meant being the most admired and revered king of Israel and so much so that Jesus Christ himself came from his bloodline.

We do not laugh because we have developed all these laughter depressants like pride, embarrassment, fear, rejection, humiliation, pain and criticism. We are taught now keep your composure, stay in control, and do not act foolish. So we keep all of this tightly bottled inside of us and it causes us pain, stress and much tension.

Laughter is a tension reliever. It is good for us. It gives us a good workout inside and out, of which you can actually see the benefits. It promotes a healthy attitude. A study conducted by Vanderbilt University reported that a couple of hours of laughing a day can actually burn 10 to 20 percent more calories[2]. So if you want a complete workout, add laughter to your regime, there are no side effects. Go ahead and laugh out loud.

Pediatricians' suggest a baby giggles for the first time at about nine weeks of age. Between a child's 3 to 4 months of age, touch and sound make a baby laugh. By the age of 10 months an infant will seek out laughter, usually through games like peek-a-boo or just looking at the silly faces that

---

[2] Plaktin, Charles Stuart, "*A Few Unique Ways to Burn Extra Calories*", KVal.com, January 9, 2008

mom or dad make.[3] This is a natural part of human development.

According to an article reported in Psychology Today the average 4 year-old laughs 300 times a day. By the age 40 and adult laughs 4 times.[4] What happened to your other 296 laughs? Some of you I can ask what happened to your 300 laughs per day? You are pretty boring and pretty unhappy to say the least.

Jesus Christ says in Matthew 18:3, "Most certainly I tell you, unless you turn, and become as little children, you will in no way enter into the Kingdom of Heaven". We have made this a religious statement, but Jesus is saying children do not question a whole lot. If you say come on jump in normally they will. Children are carefree and trusting, so they will enter into God's way of doing things without hesitation. If

you train them as children, (God's way of doing things); as far as seeking God first and His kingdom all these other

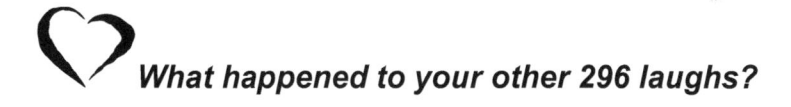

What happened to your other 296 laughs?

---

[3] Mccarthy, Laura Flynn, *"Is Your Baby Smiling"*, Parenting, 2013
[4] Gerloff, Pamela, *"Are You Meeting Your Laugh Quota?"*, Psychology Today, June 21, 2011

things will be added to you, they won't have to go through a lot of stuff to be convinced. They will just believe it.

But just like anything else, society has its way of doing things that contradicts God's way; that we have to unlearn. The minute we enter in school, we are thrown into this structured environment and we are told stop acting silly. Wipe that smile off your face girl and grow up.

So we are taught everything in life should be viewed very seriously and not lightheartedly. If you view it lightheartedly then society says something is wrong with you. We grow up and get jobs and society is still telling us, do not laugh, take this job very seriously and spend all your time working to get ahead and not spending any quality time playing or having fun with your family.

You would think that the church's attitude toward laughter would be different, that laughter would be promoted in our churches. You think... take a closer look. We find that you cannot use fun, laughter and Christian all in the same sentence. We think God is going to strike us down if we do not walk around with low looking faces at all times. Wrong!

I had four older brothers (my brother George drowned the summer of my freshmen year going into high school). My 2nd to the oldest brother Jeremiah(that we call Jerry) lived life like there was no tomorrow. After becoming an adult I would find myself saying, "why doesn't he grow up". Jerry joined the military and we wouldn't hear from him in years.

Evaluate yourself first before judging others
He was living life and having fun doing it. His living life so carefree bugged me. I was the perfectionist of the family and what society dictated I wanted to go right down the list (you know a Pharisee – thank God for deliverance). We do not even recognize why we are the way we are. After researching about tendencies of children who had parents that had co-dependencies I had to evaluate myself. Some children simulate the traits of the parent(s) with the co-dependencies and live carefree and reckless. Other children show traits of perfectionism as they do not want to be they say, "like their parents". What is ironic is they both are unhealthy and going undetected and undiagnosed would have the perfectionist to think they have it right and they need to help the one who is living life carefree (chuckle).

A few months before our mother was diagnosed with breast cancer, she called me hysteric because my brother Jerry was involved in an accident. When we arrived at the hospital things really didn't look promising and he had lost three of his limbs. I can remember that day, as I heard my mother talking to God, *"You didn't give me one child to die and I not know where they will spend eternity so it cannot be his time to go"*. I can even chuckle about this now because I didn't know the LORD then like I know him now, and I remember thinking, "momma you can't talk to God like that". Of course you can when you have relationship with Him and you have trusted God with every part of your being and your life.

On one of the visits to the hospital I recall standing in Jerry's room and only the two of us were there. He was pretty low, and he told me *if he had legs he would have jumped out of the window last night.* His room was on the 10th floor. I started jumping up and down and clapping my hands and thanking God! Can you imagine how he was looking at me, like woman have you lost your mind? He said *"Did you hear me"*, I said *"yes"* and kept right on dancing and said *if you had legs you wouldn't be here.* He started laughing and said *you are crazy*. I could see the *Spirit* of life come back over him and in him again. Jerry had made me laugh so many times before as a child now it was my time to return the favor.

<u>Laughter could save you</u>

I have never found myself saying to Jerry grow up again, because I realized that his carefree spirit is what gave him the attitude to accept what had happened to him. His attitude and spirit of laughter is what saved his life. Many couldn't have endured what he has endured. So I thank God through any situation he can demonstrate that all things can work together for your good, for those who love the Lord and are willing to let Him work them out. Jerry now spends time at the V.A. Hospital encouraging veterans that life is worth living and not having legs can't dictate who you are because who you are is living in a dirt suit. I am proud of him because he helped me to discard the weight of perfectionism and helped me realize it's okay to laugh at yourself even in the worst of times.

Since that time and dealing with my own ordeals I realize I too love to laugh, but found myself being overwhelmed with the things around me. I had cried more than I had laughed. I had complained more than gave thanks. I had torn down rather than built up. Hurting people really do hurt people and when you are empty and void you want everyone else to have that same drama going on.

I had shut myself off rather than be open and giving. Shutting off laughter is not healthy, it brings about physical and emotional side effects. Let's name a few; stress, anxiety, emotional trauma, psychological trauma, insomnia, heart problems, weight loss or weight gain and brings on other physical and emotional conditions as well. But guess what little antidote God naturally built inside of us to combat all those things I mentioned earlier. Laughter! Laughter does a soul good like a medicine.

Learn to laugh! Have you ever seen people that walk around with the countenance of sour grapes? There is nothing that could ever please them. That nothing ever seems to be going their way and they are always going through some crisis. You feel like if they could only smile even a half smile, things definitely would get better.

Melodies of Laughter

Laughter is contagious though, just like a smile, try it sometimes. You realize that you will have to transform your mind and have to learn to laugh again.

Search deep inside yourself and find the childlike attitude toward things. I thank God for my daughter Ashton that has a carefree spirit like her Uncle Jerry but she laughs at everything including herself. She does not beat up on herself if she cannot do something. She does not talk down to herself if she does not get it right the first time. I have often prayed that she will all the days of her life, have the spirit of happiness and laughter.

I do not know where you are right now, I do not know if laughing seems childish and immature to you. I do not know if you feel like you have nothing to laugh about. I do not know if your back is so against the wall that if you laughed you may get pinned there. I do not know what society has taught you and what pain your experiences have left you believing. But I do know Jesus did come that you might have life and have it more abundantly. I know He does not want you to worry or be anxious for anything.

What brings a smile to your face? What makes you laugh? Whatever it is, you should find time to promote this into your life. Let's raise the statistics on the number of times a day you laugh. Just think if you laughed three hundred times a day with your children or grandchildren what wonderful melodies your homes would make.

I worked with this guy whose office was next door to mine. He laughed from his belly, I mean right from his inner-self. When he laughed it echoed through the walls. I did not know what he was laughing about, but I found myself, smiling and even laughing sometimes when I heard him laugh. It was so rich and so complete that it touched every heart that would hear its music.

Where do you measure? Do you laugh? Do you promote laughter by speaking lightheartedly to others? They may need a good laugh today? Have any of you ever laughed so hard that you actual cried. Doesn't it feel good to you?

I want to challenge you to laugh more! The world is filled with such negative things, that we have to be the light, the salt but also the laughter for the world today. Smile be happy!

Key 5 notes:

Chapter 6
I Can, I Will and I Must

I am more than a conqueror
~ Romans 8:37

You want to go forward but something keeps you trapped. You want to be an overcomer, but it seems you get so far and the situation overtakes you. The children of Israel were slaves to the Egyptians. God gave them a leader that would lead them into the Promised Land. God fed them, clothed them, protected them and even parted the Red Sea for their safety, but as soon as the miracles were gone, they could not live in the everyday trust of God to supply their needs and provide for them. As bad as slavery was, some wanted to go back to slavery because they were comfortable with the familiar. Some would settle for the two sips of water, the crumbs of bread and the fate the Egyptians had chosen for them…it's okay.

But it is not okay. You cannot live in a cycle of worry, fear and bondage. You must trust that you can do all things through Christ Jesus who strengthens you. Before you can conceive this, you have to believe this in your heart.

God's word says, "So a man thinks so is he". So if you think you are a looser, you are a no body, you are the least, you cannot do this or that, guess what? You will have what you believe.

Proverbs 18:21, it says, *"Death and life is in the power of the tongue"*. We grew up hearing the nursery rhyme "Sticks and stones may break my bones, but words will never hurt me". Wrong! Words can kill you. Words can choke the life and dreams right out of you. Words can have you in bondage your entire life. Words can also knock you down and keep you in such low esteem that you cannot see your way out.

So what are you saying right now, what have you been speaking lately? Are you speaking life or death on yourself, family, your marriage, your health, your wealth, your job, your neighborhood or your current situation? Do you realize you are held to your words? Jeremiah 1 says, *"God will watch over His word to make them good"*.

♡ ***Words can kill you. Words can choke the life and dreams right out of you. Words can have you in bondage your entire life.***

Talking about the children of Israel; I am also reminded of the story in Numbers 13. Moses gathered the leaders from the twelve tribes of Israel to go scope (look at and observe) the land they were promised. In order to go look at something one of the necessary tools to have are eyes.

The twelve spies' only mission was to go scope out the land, take inventory on all the good stuff they would possess, and to bring back a report. This way the ones left behind, would be able to hear and see with physical evidence that the land contained all God had promised. The spies scoped out the land. Moses asked the twelve leaders for their reports. In the story ten gave a bad report. This tells you alot about why the children of Israel wondered in the wilderness for so long. Just look at their leaders. Where you lead me I will follow. The report was supposed to be a synopsis on the goods they would possess, how the land was blessed, and how if God promised them this land then they were well able to have it! But instead the report went something like "there are giants". Yes it's beautiful, but there are giants. Yes Canaan is flowing with milk and honey, but there are giants.

If you send your best, the leaders, the warriors, the most experienced and they come back saying we look like grasshoppers, can you imagine what the children's reactions would be? Exactly right! ... A lot of crying, murmuring and complaining.

Some key points to be derived from this:
Be careful in what you hear. Guard your heart with all diligence. If you hear it and receive it then it is written on your heart and an image is formed in your mind. The children of Israel saw themselves as weaklings. They saw themselves defeated and they saw themselves as not measuring up to possess the land God had promised.

As a result of what they heard, they cried, murmured and complained. They found themselves saying, "we will not make it to the Promise Land". And every person that said this or received this in their heart did not make it into the Promise Land. Not only guard your heart from what you

♡ *Be careful in what you hear. Guard your heart with all diligence. If you hear it and receive it...then it is written on your heart and image is formed in your mind.*

hear, watch the company you keep. Enough negative talk and bad reports can cause you to buy into such nonsense. People that sit around all day complaining, whining and feeding you with a lot of "you can't" are really saying "I don't want you to". Try to avoid them if you can.

I did not mention what happened to the other two leaders that Moses sent to spy out the Promised Land. Caleb and Joshua also made an observation of the Promised Land, but their response went like this, *"Oh we are well able to take these guys and possess the land that was promised to us"*.

Every time I hear this, I just leap for joy! All twelve leaders were looking at the same exact situation, but they came back with two different reports. I established earlier that a requirement for spying out the land would be eyesight, so I would think since Moses sent the leaders that all 12 leaders had eyesight.

<u>Vision</u>
But only two of the leaders had vision, which allowed them to look inside themselves, and see the promises of God that were written on their hearts and that was *"we will possess*

the Promise Land". Vision sees past the circumstance and focuses on the intended results. Eyesight will only allow you to see that which is staring you straight in the face. This image they had in them was formed from the words spoken to them by Moses and they wrote them on their hearts. Anytime doubt would arise they would refer to the words written on their hearts. Two people can hear/see the same thing but get different results. Why? One sees themselves there and the other hopes they can get there? Unless you can put vision behind your hope (which is faith activated) that is all you have is hope!

Our eyes are only the objects that we see through. It is not what we see. What we see is derived from what is established in our hearts. I could ask two people to describe a dog to me. I would get two different descriptions and the descriptions would be derived from the person's image of a dog that is inside of them. If you had a bad experience with a dog and considered them vicious, then your image of a dog would be different than one who had a dog as a childhood pet.

♡ ***Vision sees past the circumstance and focus on the intended results.***

Our images are based on past experiences. These images could have been formed from fear, abuse, and neglect. So we can see that what we have inside of us, determines what we see. Parents this is how you develop positive self-esteem in your children by building a positive image inside out.

If you give people something nice, but the images they have of themselves are broken, bruised and low, they will shrink that nice thing down to the image that they have inside of themselves. So you have to work on building up the images inside of them. You cannot do this with a one-time quick fix. You have to constantly apply God's word to their heart to create the right images.

When you get the truth on something it does bring liberation. When you are suffering because of an issue you do not need to hear about the issue, but you need the healing words of truth to speak to your life.

1 Timothy 1:7 states, *"God did not give us a Spirit of fear, but of Power, Love and a sound mind"*. Once you get the true revelation of God's word you no longer look at the situation

the same. Your attitude changes about what has happened in the past, which lets you know the future, can be better.

This does not magically appear. We have to work at these things. But we must remember I can, I must and I will work on them.

What is faith?

Jesus said (Luke 17:6 and Matthew 17:20) *"If you had the faith as a mustard seed, you might say"*... We have made this religious by emphasizing that if we had faith the size of a mustard seed then our prayers would be answered. We focused so much on the size of the mustard seed and we have heard entire sermons taught about *"it only requires just a little bit of faith"* which is true.

But this is not what this scripture is saying God's word said if you had faith *as* a, not faith *of* a; both are conjunction words. *As* means taking on the characteristics like something else. *Of* implies it is the object spoken about or referenced. *As* a mustard seed is saying like a mustard seed. *Of* a mustard seed would say that faith is a mustard seed. Is faith a mustard seed? No, it is saying faith as a mustard seed, which is comparing it to a mustard seed. But we miss the key point to this, if we had the faith as a mustard seed, what would we do? We might say. We might say what? So obviously there is some relationship to this mustard seed and saying. Can a mustard seed speak normally? No; mustard seeds do not talk, so let's discover the relationship. What would be the purpose of a mustard seed or any seed for this matter? Seeds are to be planted. The purpose of planting seed is what? We plant seeds to reap a harvest. So Jesus is saying if you had faith as a mustard seed you might say…

So what are you saying, reveals what are you planting in your heart, because whatever you plant will reap a harvest.

The mustard seed's size still emphasizes it is small. But even when you plant a small seed or when you start off speaking a little word it will grow up and produce a maximum harvest.

Take this faith as a mustard seed and say; the relationship to seeds is to say. When you say something what are you saying it with? You speak with words. So we have to speak words and we have to plant these words. The ground in which we plant our words is our heart. If we plant words in our hearts what do we expect to receive? It should be a harvest from words we wrote on our hearts and it will yield fruit (image) Whether good or bad what our mouth speaks is written on our hearts.

If you get enough word in your heart about overcoming the circumstance (the mountain) you can form image to see past the circumstance and you can overcome it. The word will break that negative image you have and make it disappear. You release image with words. It is exactly how God created the heavens and earth He spoke Word, which produced the image of that which He had inside Himself.

What will the image have in it? The image will have the detail, the blueprint, the picture and the expected results of what the word that was sown had in it. The word will manifest itself to be what image was spoken.

♡ *If you get enough word in your heart about overcoming the circumstance (the mountain) you can form image to see past the circumstance and you can overcome it.*

Like sowing seed, the harvest not only produces fruit, but also produces more of the same seed in the fruit, so you can sow more seeds. The word will produce image. And the final result will look like the word that was spoken.

If you get enough of the word planted in you it will uproot that doubt, fear, strife and whatever the adversary is using to make you feel you cannot achieve your purpose.

Changing the image inside you

To change the image inside you, you must speak to your circumstances. In Mark 11:12-25, Jesus Christ and His disciples were walking to Bethany and they were hungry. They passed a fig tree. The tree is planted, the tree has roots (obviously it is living), the tree has branches, the tree has leaves, but the tree does not have figs. But the ultimate purpose or maximum potential from a fig tree is to produce figs. If this tree's purpose is to produce figs and it is not, it is not doing what it is designed to do and because it does not bear figs, you find no more seed in this tree. From the fruit comes the seed. So if there is no seed there is no more potential to bear fruit.

When creation is not doing what it is created to do what is its purpose for existence? Jesus Christ knew the sole purpose of the fig tree was to bear figs. On this specific day in time Jesus and His disciples would walk by this tree and would be hungry, but the tree was not producing what it was created to produce. So Jesus' response was to curse the fig tree. Jesus did not curse all fig trees, but this specific one because this tree was not being what it was supposed to be and that is to produce figs. And since it was not bearing fruit it had no potential in being a fig tree because it was not bearing figs. How can you be a fig tree and never produce figs? We know a tree by the fruit it bare.

Jesus and His disciples go on where they are going and on the next morning they come past the same fig tree and the tree has died at the roots. In essence the tree is withered, the leaves are brown, and there is no life left. If Jesus would have said, leaves you are cursed, the leaves would have fallen off and died, but the tree would still have life because the life support, which is the roots were still intact. But by Jesus saying, *"No man eat fruit from you henceforth forever"*, He disconnected the life source that was underground at the roots where the tree was nourished. Christ simply doomed the fig tree to perpetual fruitlessness, i.e., death.

What's the root cause?

This should give you revelation about that situation in your life holding you in bondage. You have been speaking to the leaves, the stems, the bark, but you need to speak to the roots, if you kill it at the roots, it will die. Some of you have been talking to your symptoms, talking to the surface and never getting the root. That is why situations in your life you thought you had overcome years ago, you find out when a similar crisis arise, you freak out all over again. Speak to the poverty and lack in your life, not "that you cannot get these bills paid", but instead speak, "you do not owe any man but to love him".

Jesus demonstrated this with the fig tree to let us know the authority our words have. Jesus did not camp out there all night, dig up the tree and see if the roots were dying. Jesus released His words and with His faith, He knew the tree was dead. The tree was dead the instant His words were released. It took a while for the manifestation to take place in the natural, but in the spiritual realm it happened instantly. It took a while for what was taking place in that unseen realm to be seen. The tree was dead under the ground, but the evidence needed to manifest through the leaves, the bark, the stems and the flowers. And guess what? It did.

♡ **Summary:** *Speak to the mountain, whatever that may be in your life and say what it is you want, not what you see.*

> I am a more than a conqueror
>
> I am the head not the tail
>
> I am above only and not beneath
>
> I can do all things through Christ Jesus who strengthens me
>
> I do have purpose
>
> I can, I must and I will be an over comer and I will start today!

Key 6 notes:

Chapter 7
Victorious

I am more than a conqueror
~ Romans 8:37

In the introduction I told you I couldn't find chapter seven and the Holy Spirit told me to rewrite the chapter. Earlier I found the search for this chapter frustrating, but now I find it refreshing because when I look back over the past 14years that is exactly what has happened I rewrote the chapter.

<u>Process of getting there</u>

In 2000, I started taking classes at One In Christ Bible College, Greensboro, North Carolina, and one of the instructors, Angela invited me to her home for a Friday night Bible Study. A few months passed after the invite before I got enough courage to attend. My daughter Ashton (12 at the time) and I sat in my car across from her house and observed ladies as they went into Angela's home. Finally I heard the quiet voice of the Holy Spirit say "go in". I got enough courage to get out the car and gesture for Ashton to follow. We got to the door and it opens to a courteous smile as we find women sitting on the floor and some sitting in chairs in Angela's den. Ashton and I finds a spot on the floor and positioned ourselves to listen. Angela begin to talk about each women was invited by God as He wanted to care for their "souls". As I listened to the Word coming forth I began to weep, it was like someone took a top off the lid to my soul and stuff I had stored or never voiced came pouring out.

I had to face the fact that my marriage was a mess and that my previous husband had a substance abuse problem. I had to face the fact that I couldn't make him stop and only God could. I had to face the fact that he had to want to fight the demons that were tormenting not only his life but his family as well. I had to face the fact that even if I had planned it all out how I wanted it be, it doesn't always end up that way. I had to face the fact that even though I was still in the mess to make me feel better, I kept telling myself it was for the sake of my child because you can get comfortable even in your mess.

I didn't realize the majority of the women had left Angela's home as my daughter and I lay on her floor me in a pool of tears and Ashton in the peace that this home brought her. As I lifted my head Angela began to minister to me, no you don't understand, she ministered to my soul. She talked to the very issues that had my soul aching. I sat in amazement because I had wondered earlier how could the "church" folks walk by me Sunday after Sunday (even if I was teaching Sunday School, singing on Praise Team, attending classes in the Bible College) and not discern that my soul hurt, my very soul ached. Finally Ashton and I made our way back to our car and to our home. I knew something happened to me that night and Ashton and I made our way there many Friday nights to follow.

Women came to this Friday night Bible Study just as they were, all loving Christ with all their heart, all seeking more of God, all knowing they had specific ministry purpose, but had found life challenging issues choking their souls. Out of this Friday night gathering the Soul Care Ministry was birthed. This ministry team is led by Angela and her husband Doug. I am so blessed that God could take my desperation lying on their floor to make me a part of this ministry that cares for the "souls" of others. We no longer meet in Angela's den, but God has given us a platform to minister to women's souls.

I discovered once you have survived a great test, challenge, obstacle, sickness, or trial and it didn't kill you, but through the process you came out on the other side humble, more mature, grateful, and giving God glory – then you need to tell your sister/brother what you did to get through it! Once we realize the test isn't only for us, we will be able to go through the process and take the keys and hand them off to the next person.

My philosophy is, if it took me 12 years to get through this issue it definitely shouldn't take you that long because I want to give you the key to success so you can unlock the door and walk on through!

The road to recovery

One thing led to another and my ex-husband made some decisions about his family that left my daughter and I devastated. We left our home with the clothes we had on our backs, taking things of sentimental value more than possessions. We found ourselves in the home of a close friend where we slept for 14 hours. The tears wouldn't stop flowing from my eyes because I felt someone had reached inside of my heart, pulled it out with their hands and left me to bleed to death. I told you I had met my ex-husband at seventeen and we married when I finished college. I had suffered the grief and agony of losing both parents and now I was grieving again like the loss of a loved one that was still living. This reminds me to let you know "*soul ties*" are real and when they are joined either in marriage or not that the separating of the two brings about some strange emotions.

Each day I woke up determined to survive another day and help my daughter to cope as now she was in high school. We had our own place and life was different but we could breath. We could laugh. We could dance. We could cry. We could rest. Oh how we could rest! When you are in a war zone you don't realize how your soul, spirit, or body doesn't get the proper rest. You may lie down and sleep but you, may not be getting rest!

He called me preacher
I was still attending the Bible College and finally realized some of my emptiness was coming from me not accepting what I had heard years prior. I heard the Lord ask me to preach also in 1999 but having so much I was dealing with then, I tried to barter with God. I began in 1999 to go out and "speak" so I called myself motivational speaker. After I would speak people would comment, "You certainly sound like a preacher", so I decided to change my title to inspirational speaker. In 2004, God kept me reading this passage of Scripture:

>Ezekiel 2: *"³ He said: "Son of man, I am sending you to the Israelites, to a rebellious*

nation that has rebelled against me; they and their ancestors have been in revolt against me to this very day. ⁴ The people to whom I am sending you are obstinate and stubborn. Say to them, 'This is what the Sovereign LORD says.' ⁵ And whether they listen or fail to listen—for they are a rebellious people—they will know that a prophet has been among them. ⁶ And you, Son of man, do not be afraid of them or their words. Do not be afraid, though briers and thorns are all around you and you live among scorpions. Do not be afraid of what they say or be terrified by them, though they are a rebellious people. ⁷ You must speak my words to them, whether they listen or fail to listen, for they are rebellious. ⁸ But you, son of man, listen to what I say to you. Do not rebel like that rebellious people; open your mouth and eat what I give you (NIV)."

<u>Just do what God asked you to do</u>

I finally yielded to God's voice when He told me, A rose is still a rose called by any other name. Call yourself motivational speaker, exhorter, an inspirational speaker. But I call you preacher. He calls me preacher. Every time I hear it I'm just as amazed God called me, and He called me preacher. Well the rest is history. In 2004, I gave my proclamation and presented myself to the senior elder and to the pastor of the church I was attending. Since I already was attending Bible College, my next steps were ministry classes. I was already teaching King's Children Church and one of the greatest and humbling experiences I ever had. You say you are a preacher, well help these children understand what you are talking about. I was elevated to teach an adult School of Discipleship class. First it shows you how much you don't know and second, it shows you God will walk with you every step of the way. I studied and grew in this class as it challenged me to eat the scroll as God had told me to do earlier.

A lot of things had changed in my life including my place of employment. I was still in the computer technology field, but God was elevating me even in my professional career. I used my position in the work place or market place to walk out the goodness of Jesus. My countenance had changed, my outlook had changed, and my soul had healed. One of my coworkers invited me to her church to preach during their Women's Conference. I accepted and recall speaking about *"What Does Love Have to Do With It?"*

Inner vows are made with your head not your heart
Be careful about making inner vows as I made one "I will never marry again" because it speaks from the head and not from the heart. God knew in my heart I loved being married, I loved the institution of marriage, and I loved working with a life mate to help meet the plans God had for us. I asked God to heal my heart and make me whole from vowing something with my mouth that my heart didn't mean. I also asked God to forgive me because I had made a vow in a previous marriage but it had ended in hurt and pain. I asked God to forgive my ex-husband for all the pain he brought to our home. I asked God to forgive me for the part I played in that hurt and pain. Then I asked God to help us forgive each other. I pray for my ex-husband's wholeness, that he is well, that he is delivered and set free from every stronghold that wants to keep him bound.

What Does Love Have to Do With It?
I often tell the women I minister to when I went to the church to preach at the Women's Conference, I didn't go to look for a husband I went to preach the gospel, and love has everything to do with it. Christ so loved me that He wants the best for me even when I don't know what that is. I wouldn't have imagined accepting that preaching

engagement and then coming back again for another preaching engagement would put me in front of my husband (and he was the pastor) but it did!

I chuckle now because I had never seen myself as a pastor's wife, but God did (still a lot to learn). God will use all of your experiences to prepare you for where you are going. On July 7, 2007, God restored me and blended Ashton and I with Jack and his four children. We don't refer to our children as "step" nor do our children refer us as "step", we are "mom" and "dad". I am so grateful that Jesus Christ Himself was a part of a blended family as Joseph was not his earthly father and he had siblings that were "step" by the world's standards but they were family.

Where Do I fit?

"Change isn't change until it has changed", probably would be a great mantra for me as change has been my story. Marrying my pastor and being a minister not only affected my spiritual journey, but it meant changes physically as well…Changing where we lived, changed our church, and changed where I worked. Ashton had matriculated through high school and had gone to college. It required a lot of trial and error to find out where did I fit? Trying to find out what did being a pastor's wife entail. Trying to blend families together so no one was feeling they were losing anything, but they all were gaining a lot. Trying to stay true to myself so I wouldn't lose Pam in the process. I must say I have matured from the young girl that married before right out of college and had heard about God. Now I know God. I'm still learning my way as a pastor's wife, but most of all learning my life as a wife as in when we know better we should do better.

What's in your bags?

If you are coming from previous marriages or relationships you are taking that baggage with you. A huge key to success is realizing you have baggage (what liberation and freedom comes with actually acknowledging you have baggage). I said this because some of enter new relationships expecting certain things to take place and when they don't we have a tendency to put the blame on the other individual. If we are honest with ourselves, we brought our baggage to the marriage and the other person brought their baggage so we have a lot of baggage that needs to be sorted. Some things need to be tossed, some kept, some upgraded, and some just opened to see what it consists of. This baggage can be good, bad, or indifferent. This baggage can contain trauma, drama, pain, shame, ugliness, bitterness, resentment, sadness, happiness, peace, and the laundry list can go on and on. But whatever we have we carry it into the relationship and so does the other person. When I say relationships it doesn't have to be husband – wife; boyfriend – girlfriend. It can be mother – daughter; brother – brother; sister – sister; pastor – congregant; shepherd – sheep; friend – friend. Either way, we all have issues based on past experiences that cause us to handle these relationships a certain way. If you have been hurt by girlfriends in the past, it will be a little more difficult for you to trust girlfriends in the future. If you have been in a relationship in the past and your husband and/or boyfriend dogged you, abused you and hurt you, it will be difficult for you to trust in the future. This is how the luggage gets filled with the stuff we carry around. You may no longer be in the relationship with the person, but may sleep with them daily because you have a ball and chain around your ankle dragging them around with you. When the new person says anything that sounds like something the past person said, it's going to take you to that place.

If you are in any relationship trying to fulfill a void it will not happen because the only one that can fulfill that void is

Christ. If you want to save yourself some time and trouble do not put false expectations on people because they cannot be your Savior! A broken person cannot connect to a whole person or another broken person and think that will make you whole.

<u>What makes you whole?</u>

- A broken person must acknowledge they are broken.
- A broken person should be crying out to the Lord to show them their issues and give them the strength to do something about what is revealed
- To be made whole requires an open mind and heart
- To be made whole requires the Word of God
- To be made whole requires a touch from God
- To be made whole requires applying life changing revelation for your future
- To be made whole the transformation becomes a lifestyle you embrace
- To be made whole requires you doing something different than what you are accustomed to
- To be made whole you must guard, protect, and keep your heart once the wholeness/healing comes

- To be made whole the foundational key to becoming effective in any relationship is discovering and capturing of a sense of purpose for your own life
- To be made whole you must SHARE your love with someone else

Key 7 notes:

Conclusion

When we are open in pursuing a *"pure heart"* it is the first step to receiving it. This process should never stop. We should always be seeking to be better and keeping our hearts clear from contamination.

Key 1: Spirit

♡ Summary - Who are you? One may ask... What will you say? Look inside out before you answer. Will you go before God? Will you say, "I want to be whole; I want to be complete in every area of my life".

You are a spirit that is housed in a body and you have emotions or sensors that should be connected to your spirit that discerns between good and evil.

Your mind needs to be transformed so you can be made whole. You cannot change where you have come from, but starting from this moment forward you can help shape where you are going. You can feed your heart (spirit), mind and body with good stuff and as a result you can be better equipped to fulfill the purpose God has for you!

Key 2: Purpose

Summary - Why did you come to earth? What is your assignment? Have you stopped to ask yourself these questions? The whole course of our being here is about purpose and your Spirit will continue to seek that purpose in you until this journey.

1. Spend time each day paying attention to yourself. What are those things you do just naturally without thinking? What are those things you can do that you lose track of time doing?
2. You need to know your Creator
3. What are those things you do that you prefer not doing? This tells you what are learned talents and skills versus God given gifts and talents.
4. Do proper research. Need to invest time in self. Study God's Word and spend quality time with your Creator seeking His will for your life.
5. Develop techniques to record or document vision. Keep a journal, carry a small tape recorder or just keep a small pad and pencil. As things are revealed to you

through God's Word, through God, through dreams, through visions or through people record them.
6. Do not be afraid to act out on that unction that comes to you. Do not be afraid to try things. Do not be afraid to step out on faith, even when you get it wrong, at least you tried. There's a saying that goes, "I did not do it wrong this makes just 10,001 things I tried that did not work". After a while there is a process of elimination.
7. Realize the Spirit knows why He sent you, as you get closer to your purpose, He will speak clearer, it will become real.

Key 3: Pure Heart

♡ Summary - How do I seek a pure heart?

1. You have to talk to God. You have to spend quality time with God your Creator to find out what is of Him and what is not.
2. When things are revealed to you from God (and they will be) admit it, do not deceive yourself and say, that is not me. You want to be whole and the sooner you can admit and confess all of your junk the sooner your healing are on the way.

3. Once an issue is revealed, ask God to heal you and what do you do from there.

Key 4: Love

Summary - Matthew 22:37-40: "Love the Lord your God with all your heart and with all your soul and with all your mind, This is the first and greatest commandment. And the second is like it: 'Love your neighbor as yourself'". It took me a while to get the understanding to this Scripture, but it is saying, learn to love God who is love first with all three parts of you. Once you learn how to love from Love then you can love others. And if you love others the way God intended there isn't need for all the other commandments because you would not be doing anything to anyone to bring them hurt, pain, or harm.

To get this love, you must accept love that is unconditional with no strings attached because it has been paid for in full. To accept this love, it requires a much deeper revelation to sink in rather than you just getting goose bumps. You must understand the depths and the widths of God's LOVE.

Jesus really does love you like that. How do I mean this? I mean you have to experience His love with your heart instead of your head.

There is a part of you that truly does want to please God, though you feel you will never get there. The harder you try to do it right, to be nice to go that extra mile is the same time you keep on messing up. So you become frustrated with yourself, but keep on trying.

It is not by works, not by your efforts, but because of the Love of Christ and His love alone, is why He died on a Cross just for you. Can you just let go and let God love you? Can you let Him love you because He's God and He chooses to love you just the way you are? Will you let Him love you right where you are? Will you let him love you so much that every tear you have shed He collects them to refresh you with later. Every stumble you will make, He is right there to clean and wipe the wound and put His band-aid of love on it and kiss the boo-boo. God loves you!

Key 5: Laughter

♡ Summary - Where do you measure? Do you laugh? Do you promote laughter by speaking lightheartedly to others? They may need a good laugh today? Have any of you ever laughed so hard that you actually cried. Doesn't it feel good to you?

I want to challenge you to laugh more! The world is filled with such negative things that we have to be the light, the salt, but also the laughter for the world today.

I do not know where you are right now. I do not know if laughing seems childish and immature to you. I do not know if you feel like you have nothing to laugh about. I do not know if your back is so against the wall that if you laughed you might get pinned there. I do not know what society has taught you and what pain your experiences have left you believing. I do know Jesus did come that you might have life and have it more abundantly. I know He does not want you to worry or be anxious for anything.

What brings a smile to your face? What makes you laugh? Whatever it is, you should find time to promote this into your life. Let's raise the statistics on the number of times a day you laugh. Just think if you laughed 300 times a day with your children or grandchildren what wonderful melodies your homes would make.

Key 6: I Can

Summary *Speak to the mountain, whatever that may be in your life and say what it is you want, not what you see.*

I am more than a conqueror
I am the head not the tail
I am above only and not beneath
I can do all things through Christ Jesus who strengthens me
I am the righteousness of God

I do have purpose
I can, I must and I will be an over comer and I will start today!

Key 7: Victory

♡ Summary - What makes you whole? A broken person must acknowledge they are broken. A broken person should be crying out to the Lord to show them their issues and give them the strength to do something about what is revealed.

- To be made whole requires an open mind and an open heart
- To be made whole requires the Word of God
- To be made whole requires a touch from God
- To be made whole requires applying the life changing revelation
- To be made whole the transformation becomes a lifestyle
- To be made whole requires you doing something different
- To be made whole you must guard, protect, and keep your heart once the wholeness/healing comes
- To be made whole the foundational key to becoming effective in any relationship is discovering and capturing a sense of purpose for your own life

- To be made whole you must discover your personal purpose for your life and finding it will give you reason and meaning for living
- To be made whole you must SHARE love with someone else

You are victorious because only a "pure heart" knows what is true. Receiving a pure heart begins with you acknowledging that you want it and it must end with God creating it! Thank you for taking the time to go on this journey with me! May God bless you and keep you in perfect peace through Christ Jesus Our Lord. Amen! ~ Pam

The Jacksons

PAMELA STANFIELD JACKSON

Pamela (Pam) S. Jackson is an ordained elder of Citadel of Faith Christian Fellowship (CFCF), Thomasville, NC. She has a BA in Business Information Technology from Winston-Salem State University and a MBA in Leadership from Walden Walden University as well in Business Administration - Leadership. She has a Certificate in Christian Leadership from United Cornerstone School of Divinity (UCSoD) and currently pursuing a Master of Divinity Degree. She serves as minister of New Members, Young Adults, and Pureheart Ministries.

Pam is Dean of Church Business Systems at UCSoD. She teaches in-house and online courses Pam is happily married to her best friend and pastor (Citadel Ministries) and president of UCSoD, Bishop Dr. George B. Jackson. They are the proud parents of five children and three grandchildren.

You can reach Pam at www.citadeloffaith.net (Pureheart Ministries), pam-pureheart@carolina.rr.com or call 336.476.7218.

Bibliography

Fernandez, Gail, MD., *"Reactive Attachment Disorder"*, Child Development Institute LLC, 1999

Gerloff, Pamela, *"Are You Meeting Your Laugh Quota?"*, Psychology Today, June 21, 2011

Mccarthy, Laura Flynn, *"Is Your Baby Smiling"*, Parenting, 2013

Plaktin, Charles Stuart, *"A Few Unique Ways to Burn Extra Calories"*, KVal.com, January 9, 2008

Made in the USA
Charleston, SC
05 May 2016